More Praise for
STRENGTH & HONOR

This is a book for all ages - from young adults who are inter-
ested in leadership development to Executive Directors of
organizations. As a CEO, the lessons in **Strength & Honor**
remind me of the key relationship between the individuals and
the mission of our organization. These especially include the
stories about asking the right questions, discussing values and
committing to your staff. Best of all these stories are experiences we can relate to within our own lives.

> **-Bill Farkas** | CEO, Lambda Chi Alpha Fraternity Inc.

Strength & Honor captures the importance that family, church,
DeMolay and the military played in John's life....his stories are
valuable lessons youth and adults can really relate to in their
own life! John delivers a powerful book on leadership!

> **-Tom Moberly** | Executive Director,
> Northern California DeMolay Association

It is always my hope to take away a few life enriching lessons
from every leadership book I read. In **Strength & Honor**, you
get 64 lessons which will improve your life at all levels! The
stories will resonate with all types of leaders, specifically
younger generations and those who are learning to lead as
they begin their careers.

> **-Dan Nilsen** | CEO, Bishop-McCann

John Hinck is a natural born leader. In **Strength & Honor**, we
find, through John's life lessons and experiences, just how he
refined his talents to be one of the most energetic and accomplished motivational leaders of today. His true tales in this
book are refreshing and a must read for all determined leaders
of profits and nonprofits.

> **-David A. Glattly, 33°** | Active Member and
> Deputy for New Jersey Ancient Accepted Scottish
> Rite, Northern Masonic Jurisdiction, USA

STRENGTH & HONOR

64 Stories of Leadership, Character, and Values

STRENGTH & HONOR

64 Stories of Leadership, Character, and Values

John M. Hinck

Book Press™
publishing

Published in Des Moines, Iowa, by BookPress Publishing.

Publisher's Cataloging-in-Publication Data

Hinck, John M., 1967–
    Strength and honor : 64 stories of leadership, character and values / John Hinck.
    p. cm.
    ISBN 978-0-9855133-7-5
    Includes bibliographical references.

1. Hinck, John M.. 2. Leadership – Biography. 3. Military biography. 4. Leadership – Moral and ethical aspects. 5. Character. 6. Integrity 7. Success in business. 8. Conduct of life. I. Strength and honor : sixty-four stories of leadership , character , and values. II. Title.

HD57.7 .H55 2014
302.3/4092 --dc23   2014939264

First Edition

Printed in the United States of America
10 9 8 7 6 5 4 3 2 1

This book is dedicated to my mom and dad.

How you lived your lives, your personal strengths, and your character have always been my guiding lights.

CONTENTS

ACKNOWLEDGMENTS

*For giving me their ideas, laughter, and a place to grow; my older
brother: Dr. Edward Hinck, and his wife, Dr. Shelly Schaefer-Hinck*

*For his mentorship in writing, editing, book design, and publishing:
Dr. Tony Paustian*

*For lessons on how to think, speak, act, dream, listen, lead, and love:
Dorothy Hinck (grandmother), Karen Giles, and Teresa, all the Hincks,
Tom Moberly, Gene Tong, Bob Young, John-John Spolsdoff, Mike
Kennedy, Doug Reitz, the Hampton family, Scott Cooper, Jim Sullivan,
James Banta, Mike Bishop, Keith Klein, Fred Haug, Dwight McBride,
Dave Glattly, Dave Compton, Dave Smith, Eleni Wise, Loren Froomin,
Mom and Dad Froomin, Beth Johnston, Tom Labagh, Sam Williamson,
Bob and Marion Hannon, Doug Vaughn, Bridget Farris, Monsignor
Moreton, Father Fleury, Sister Mary, Father Pete, Rick Hausman,
Mary Cavanaugh, Charles Bowery, Mary-Ann Bowery, Morgan Lamb,
John Evans, Mike Swanson, John Pack, Sam Hubbard, John and Anne
MacDonald, Darrell Oenning (my first platoon sergeant), Anthony and
Celeste Cassino, Chip and Mary Retzlaff, Rick Boysen, Frank Ippolito,
Mike Klingele, Laura Reidenbach, Mark Arden, Brad and Carla
Barker, Randy and Jill Boucher, Joel Smith, Brian Dunn, Andre
Cardoza, Ed Adams, Cory Mendenhall, Frances Ferry, Carl Coffman,
John Lindsay, Oliver Hunter, Rick Rife, Patrick Laidlaw, Warren
Phipps, Perry Wiggins, Brad Nelson, Bill Morris, Mike Anthanasakis,
Preston Pysh, Arnie Albornoz, Tom Dirienzo, Cameron Gallagher,
Chris Dishong, Jeremy Mueller, Terri Sparks, Tim Marlowe, Brian
Wallace, Keith Haskin, James Lax, Steve Weber, Ron Lewis, Mike
Hauser, Ed Box, David Mann, Butch Kievenaar, John Baker, James &
Dee Thurman, Dan Nilsen, Dave Brinkerhoff, Dan Meiners, Dr. Tony
Paustian, Shannon Miller Baird, Adam Carroll, Dr. Verna Price,
Dr. Susan Larson, Dr. Sherri Turner, Deborah Yungner, Jen Polz,
Howie Dumhart, D.J. Gomez, Tasha Caess, and Scott Johnston.
I am because of you.*

CHAPTER 1

My Journey to
Strength & Honor!

Before bedtime in the Hinck household, my father read stories from the Bible and other great books to my twin brother and me. In the Army, stories were always swapped around barracks, in a motor pool, on a flight line, and during deployments. As a speaker, audiences gravitated toward the personal and military stories I shared on leadership, character, and values. Often, people preferred my military stories than the rest of the speech.

Who doesn't like good stories? They can make us laugh, smile, think, or cry. My motivation to write this book started with my family and my church in childhood. My military service and audience feedback during my keynote addresses only strengthened this motivation. As a leader in the Army, I filled 26 little green books with thousands of observations and lessons. *Strength and Honor!* is my effort to share 64 of the best leadership stories I learned from family, church, and the military.

My stories, all from the viewpoint of my over 22-year career as a military leader, will have readers thinking, laughing, smiling, and maybe even tearing up at times. Although the book takes readers on a journey from my growing up in California to Army posts at Forts Rucker,

Bragg, Leavenworth, and Hood to my deployments in South Korea, Germany, Albania, and Afghanistan, each chapter stands alone as a lesson for leadership at different levels. These include formative years (Chapter 2), entry-level leadership (Chapter 3), mid-level leadership (Chapter 4), senior-level leadership (Chapter 5), and executive-level leadership (Chapter 6). The lessons—free standing and readable in any order—are revealed through stories, which explain leadership fundamentals like setting a foundation, learning a craft, practicing standards of excellence, perfecting the art and science of command, and observing lifelong leadership.

Please enjoy *Strength and Honor!*

CHAPTER 2

Formative Years: Setting a Foundation

LESSON #1   Appreciate life, take nothing for granted, and understand why everything is relative.

The Journey of Six WWII POWs from the Philippines to California

On October 20th, 1944, General Douglas MacArthur and his forces landed in the Philippines and fulfilled his promise of "I shall return." A few days later, American forces began liberating the many POW camps near Manila. Among the survivors were six Hincks: my grandmother and family patriarch, Dorothy; my father, Ed; my aunts, Ethel and Mary Lou; and two uncles, John and Robert. After almost three years of being held captive by Japanese forces, the surviving family members boarded boats and began their new journeys. Upon arrival to San Francisco, they decided to move to Fresno due to incredibly good housing offered to POWs and internees. I remember growing up surrounded by family and extended family.

My father's family rarely talked about their final years on the islands, but when they did, it always centered on how their time as prisoners made them take nothing for granted.

They had little notice they would be captured, and no idea the internment would last over three years (my father was 18 to 21 during his time as a POW). Lack of food deteriorated their health; after, my father would eat everything on his plate, wasting nothing.

My family lost parents and friends in WWII; therefore, they spent much time together because their relationships had deeper meaning than before. They didn't want to lose those moments that mattered. They didn't laugh much during their internment, but in America, they celebrated their freedoms through light-heartedness and jokes, usually at each other's expense. Their behavior was indicative of their appreciation for life . . . that everything in life is relative. "Make the best of your circumstances, and don't complain" was a recurring phrase in the Hinck households.

I adopted this attitude in my military career. Toward the beginning of my career as an Army aviator, I attended a survival school where I experienced the challenges associated with being a POW—surviving, evading, resisting, and escaping. Hearing of my schooling, my father quipped, "At 74, after three years in a prison camp, a few days in a survival course would seem like summer camp." From that perspective, I understood everything in life is relative.

All of my deployments were challenging. In Albania, the water table was about a foot below the surface making foot and vehicle movement slow and difficult. In Iraq, the dust storms and heat posed constant challenges for Soldiers and aviators. In Afghanistan, the winters nearly caused a stoppage of action on all sides, and the high mountain altitudes made operations a task. Yet if my father could survive three years as a POW, then I could surely make it through a few months of war.

After a few deployments, whenever someone asked how I was doing, my normal response was "I am doing great... life could be worse, but I have food in my stomach, a warm place to sleep, a place to call home, and no one is shooting at me." Leaders understand that life should be appreciated, nothing should be taken for granted, and everything is relative.

LESSON #2 Successful people possess strong grit, a blend of unwavering courage and persistence.

Dorothy Hinck and the Hinck Bill

Just saying "grandmother" conjures images of a strong woman, wise in counsel and strong in soul. Add character, courage, persistence, and long, black hair atop a sturdy Chinese-Scottish woman who speaks five languages (Cantonese, Tagalog, English, Latin, and Spanish), throw in the tenacity of a bulldog, and you have my grandmother. As a young girl, Dorothy Allen Hinck grew up in Shanghai, China and struggled with early childhood health problems. She moved to the Philippines to live with relatives for the better island climate.

She met and married John H. Hinck, my grandfather

after whom I was named, who was serving in the U.S. Army on the islands. They had a great life raising their five kids. My grandfather rose through the enlisted ranks became an officer, retired near Manila, and worked for the Port Authority. When WWII arrived to the islands, life was tumultuous at best. Because of the war, my grandfather was recalled to active service but died in November 1941 from a heart attack shortly after an invasion on a Navy ship. My grandmother heard from the chaplain that her husband died, and the body was to be buried in a cemetery near Clark Air Force Base. There was no agency to assist with the funeral or provide a death certificate.

The Japanese invaded the islands in December 1941. My now-widowed grandmother and her five kids, including my father, were captured in early February 1942 and interned in prison camps. Their three-year internment in those harsh conditions ended with liberation in January 1945. In the end, the Philippines became the final resting place for over 60,000 Americans and almost 300,000 Japanese, but estimates for the cost to Filipinos neared one million[1]. The family was fortunate to survive and sought to renew their freedoms. My grandmother's courage and determination endured.

I fast-forward to San Francisco, California to the reception center where the Hincks landed. In my father's own words (as captured in the unpublished work, *The Book of Ed: My Father's POW Story*):[2]

> The immigration offices gave us a bad time. We were the last to get off of the boat. They questioned mother's claim about being American. All of us children were on the list of being Americans,

but Mother was British. Mom finally proved to the officials that she married Dad before the 1918 law was passed. Anyone who married an American in a foreign land became an American by taking his [husband's] status as an American citizen. Immigration officials complained that mom was an illegal entering the states. But your grandmother finally convinced them that she was certainly an American citizen by showing them her marriage certificate.

After immigration agents asked my grandmother to provide proof of citizenship in the form of her husband's death certificate, she replied with a stoic gaze: "As a POW for three years, where do you think I kept those kinds of papers?"

My grandmother and her children were detained until the U.S. Army could find proper documentation and until other family on the east coast could vouch for them. Ultimately, my family relocated to Fresno in the center of the San Joaquin Valley of central California.

After establishing a new home there, my grandmother filed to claim her husband's benefits such as his pay and allowances, something to which surviving spouses of military members are entitled. Her initial request was denied. To receive the compensation, the claims division within the U.S. Department of Veterans Affairs needed proof she was legally married to John Hinck, certification of his service in the U.S. Army, and documentation that he died in combat accompanied by a copy of his death certificate. Although she provided the faded marriage certificate and his Army service records, it took a while to get an actual copy of his death certificate.

After almost a year of waiting and working with several levels of government, she received an official death certificate. Her claim finally had all the proper documentation. However, the statute of limitations expired. Again, she was denied benefits. The wording of the law meant she had to claim benefits during her time as a POW, which clearly would have been impossible.

For the next three decades, my grandmother campaigned to change the law and amend the statute of limitations. She wrote over 20 letters to governmental representatives, the Department of the Army, and Veterans Affairs seeking acceptance of her rightful claim to survivor benefits. With every denial, her determination and courage strengthened. Several elected officials, specifically Representative B.F. Sisk of California, and governmental agencies assisted in giving her cause a voice.

Finally, after countless attempts spanning 31 years, on July 8, 1975, President Gerald Ford signed H.R. 2946, dubbed a "bill for the relief of Mrs. Dorothy Hinck":[3]

> Be it enacted by the Senate and House of Representatives of the United States of America in Congress assembled, That, notwithstanding the provisions of section 3010 of title 38, United States Code, or any statute of limitations, Mrs. Dorothy Hinck, widow of John Henry Hinck (XC-3,009,409) is to be held and considered to have filed a timely application for death compensation for herself and minor children within one year of the death of the said John Henry Hinck on November 24, 1941, and is to be paid the amounts due as otherwise provided in the laws administered by the Administrator of Veterans' Affairs. Approved July 8, 1975.

Subsequently, Private Law 94-14 was enacted, and future laws were amended to remove the requirement of a one-year statute of limitations. Future acceptance of claims was based on the merits of the claim. Over the 31 years she fought for her rightful benefits, she also raised five children and headed the household, so her children could have the opportunity for a better life. Despite the numerous challenges, my grandmother won her fight to change one of our nation's unjust laws. She could have given up any time amid the mounting periods of defeat. Yet my grandmother fought for what was right.

Grit is the combination of repeated persistence with unwavering courage. Today, the Hinck Bill stands as a testament to Dorothy Hinck's grit. Almost every successful person endures countless efforts with undaunted courage on a path to their own freedoms and success. Grit is what separates those who try and those who succeed. Leaders possess grit.

LESSON #3   The power to choose attitude.

"...Either way, you're going to church."

I mentioned earlier my family had a strong relationship with the Catholic Church. We attended mass every Sunday, usually the 10 a.m. service by Monsignor Moreton. Our family liked his homilies. I remember one Sunday morning I was not particularly motivated to roll out of bed and get ready to attend mass. On a second visit to my room, my father said, "You have a choice . . . you can go to church and like it, or you can go and not like it, but either way, you're going to church. Now, get up and get dressed."

In this stern yet fatherly manner, my dad was holding

me accountable to our family tradition. Although I couldn't control the family rules, I could control my attitude. I knew my left and right limits, and my father made me clearly understand I had the power of choosing my attitude within those limits. The lesson taught me to choose the right attitude regardless of the situation. I went to mass with the right attitude; I was more open to the teachings of our faith.

In life, attitude makes all the difference in how we approach life and how others see us. People tend to follow others with more positive, optimistic attitudes.

LESSON #4   Relationships matter. Trust in relationships matters more.

The Knights Templar and the Order of DeMolay

Many of the Catholic Church's teachings are influenced by history. I remember one of the Sunday morning classes when we reviewed the history of Catholicism. I learned about organizations like the Knights Templar, the Hospitallers of Jerusalem, and the Order of Malta Knights. Years later, the name of DeMolay was brought up when my best friend invited me to a dance where he promised twice as many girls as boys. That seemed like a good deal, so I went and had a blast.

The name DeMolay was familiar from my Sunday school teachings. I inquired more about the name from my friend, and he said the dance was put on by the Order of

DeMolay, which took its name from Jacques DeMolay, a Knights Templar who protected the pilgrims on their journey to Jerusalem. The modern day Order of DeMolay taught young men to live by three bulwarks—bible, flag, and schoolbooks—and seven precepts—Filial Love, Reverence for Sacred Things, Courtesy, Comradeship, Fidelity, Cleanliness, and Patriotism.[4]

The reason the dance had twice as many girls as boys was because girls attended from two organizations devoted to the character development of young women. Job's Daughters taught lessons based on the Book of Job, and Rainbow for Girls emphasized acting based on seven colors (or virtues) of love, religion, nature, immortality, fidelity, patriotism, and service. As an older teenager, I dated girls from both organizations. But it was the Order of DeMolay that had a lasting impact on my life.

The link to history, my Catholic Church, and the ideals of love of parents, brotherhood, fidelity, and patriotism fit well within the framework my father already taught me. Additionally, the organization gave me some of my best friends as well as a sense of belonging, which came at a time in my life when I most needed it. My middle brother died in 1974 of Reye's syndrome, my mother died in 1979 of cancer, my older brother was away from home at college, and my father worked as the family's sole provider. My twin brother and I did much of the cleaning, laundry, and cooking to help. As latchkey kids, my twin and I had time to fill. We did homework or played sports, but, for me, DeMolay had all that and more.

In 1983, I joined DeMolay's youth leadership fraternity. It gave me history education, athletics, camaraderie, discipline, leadership, and training. And it gave me the opportunity to meet great people. DeMolay reinforced and extended the values provided by my family and the Catholic Church. But what DeMolay did best was provide me with the value of relationships. Not only did I learn this through the historical example of Jacques DeMolay and the relationship with his brothers of the Knights Templar, but I also learned it from the relationship between the Church and the Templars.

Jacques DeMolay died due to his fidelity with his fellow Templars and broken trust with church hierarchy. The trust or fidelity between Templars resonated with me. It is the people and our relationships with them that have the greatest influence in life. I am still friends with my fellow DeMolays and incredible advisors from 30 years ago. Many of their names are in the acknowledgements of this book.

Humans are social by nature. We act based on relationships and social interactions, which sometimes seem irrational or crazy. Our actions are extensions of trust with others in our relationships. I trust others until I am given a reason to think or act otherwise. When the trust is broken, so is the relationship. As a soldier, the breach of integrity signifies a lack of trust and negates the value of the relationship. What the Church and DeMolay taught me, what the Army strengthened in me, is my belief in the importance of relationships and the value of trust.

LESSON #5 Asking the right questions ("Why?" and "What if?")

"You can't become a Eucharistic Minister"

I have always felt called to serve the Catholic faith. At one time, I considered becoming a priest but felt more of a calling to serve within the armed forces. Interestingly, the first chaplain in the U.S. Army was a Catholic priest, so a dual idea of service existed within my formative years: service to Christ and service to our nation. As a teen, losing my life seemed less of a challenge than committing to some of a priest's vows. (Kid math doesn't always make sense.) As part of my religious call to service, becoming a Eucharistic Minister (now called a Lay Minister of the Eucharist or LME for short) seemed a win-win situation.

However, at 17, I was told, "You can't become a Eucharistic Minister because you have to be 18."

My response was, "Why?" Requiring an age minimum didn't make sense to me. The call to service has no age limits. My next response was, "What if I get an exception from the diocese?" I was told no one had ever done that. To me, that meant becoming an LME was within the realm of possible.

This lesson is related to the notion that "No is the beginning to YES!" It took a few months for the Bishop to grant approval. Monsignor Moreton, the head priest at Sacred Heart Church, interviewed me and endorsed me to serve in the position for the church. I became the youngest LME in the church history and went on to serve as a Lector (reading

Scripture during mass), youth minister in Club Beyond, and Parish Council President. Asking the right questions to determine what is possible is imperative to navigating the realm of the possible. Most rules have exceptions. We must ask and fight for what we want using the power of questions.

LESSON #6   Reactions to an event are more important than the events themselves.

"If it's not one thing, it's another..."

My father is well known for the phrase, "If it's not one thing, it's another." The sentence means something will always happen to present challenges. The pattern never ends. Life presents challenges, sometimes when we least expect or want them. We can't always control what happens, but we can control how we react. At times, life seems unfair: Being a POW as a teen, losing a spouse to cancer, being shot at in foreign lands, losing a job, or being upside down on a mortgage. The list continues.

How we react, though, is determined by where we focus. We can react to the event (past focus) or react to how we will adjust (future focus). What often followed my father's declaration was "focus on the future." The Army had its own way of emphasizing a focus on the future. If someone said, "life is not fair," the Army's response was, "get over it." The Army wanted Soldiers to focus on adapting. A phrase like, "We grow by the things we overcome," built upon those notions. We must act with informed initiative and in a professional manner to achieve the desired results, especially if we want to score big in life.

LESSON #7 Scoring big means doing what matters.

Professionals Don't Play Little-Kid Soccer

I played soccer as a kid. I equate little-kid soccer with having fun, whether we scored or not; we moved the ball around, and everyone was the winner. As I progressed through the levels of sports—pee-wee, little league, middle school, high school, and college—the emphasis turned more to winning. Professionals, no matter the game, are paid to win.

Scoring big and doing what matters most are keys to being successful, whether in professional soccer or the workplace. If we try to make a goal using the right moves, then we can score big. If we are being paid by tangible means (money being the most obvious) or by intangibles (love and trust), our actions and our ability to achieve the desired end goals are rewarded accordingly. Moving the ball around means acting but not necessarily doing the actions that matter; hence, we're not scoring.

I learned how to score big by doing what mattered most to become an Army helicopter pilot, specifically, an Apache helicopter pilot. I researched the heck out of everything associated with Army aviation, Army helicopter flight school, the branch of aviation, the Apache helicopter, and the path to becoming an officer. I developed an informed initiative and made a detailed plan that led to accomplishing my big dream. My objective was to make my application stand out as someone who was already scoring big and possessing the qualities of an Army aviator. Numerous methods existed to achieve this end state, and each had several steps, requirements, and qualifications. So, I wrote down all of the major decision points along the path and developed specific tasks to propel me from one point to the next. If there was knowledge I needed like for the flight entrance exam, I developed a plan to study. If there was a skill or experience I needed like flight experience, ground school, or an understanding of Army aviation, I developed a plan to acquire it. If I needed access to a program or to meet someone with decision-making power, I developed a plan to make that introduction. When the committee reviewed my Army Aviation Branch application file, I wanted it to scream Army aviator and make their decision easy.

One path to becoming an officer was through ROTC, but selection for the aviation branch was a tough cut. I had to excel in ROTC and be selected over peers who also dreamed of flying. I did what mattered in building my cadet packet to be the top choice for Army aviation. In ROTC, I sought to graduate as a Distinguished Military Graduate (DMG). I joined the Army Reserves and served in an aviation unit. I studied day and night to score high on the flight aptitude test. I enrolled in ground school and learned the fundamentals of flying. The university did not offer a degree in aviation, so I developed a unique program which merged business management, aviation ground school, and aviation weather classes to create a special major called aviation management. It all mattered.

The plan worked. I graduated a DMG, received the General George C. Marshall Award for top cadet, and was selected to become an aviation officer in the U.S. Army. I was on my way to becoming an Army aviator.

Becoming an Apache helicopter pilot, however, took four more years. After completing the Army's rotary wing qualification course, I was selected to attend the challenging aeroscout course, something the schoolhouse wanted to ensure officers would complete. I scored high in academics, but I was not selected for the Apache course.

Instead of focusing on the past event, I focused on becoming the best scout pilot. I was assigned to Fort Bragg and continued my focus. Within six months of arriving to the unit, I became a pilot-in-command as a second lieutenant. When the unit reconsolidated due to Army transformation, I was put in charge of all scout aircraft. By focusing on my present job of being the best aeroscout pilot, I exceeded expectations. Fort Bragg had one slot available in the Apache qualification course due to the transition. I was selected.

It took some time, but I continued to do what mattered most in becoming an Apache Helicopter Pilot. Leaders score big by doing what matters most in life, for family, and in the workplace.

LESSON #8   Rank and experience are not the
same; regardless of either, treat
everyone with dignity and respect.

"What's the Difference between a PFC and a 2LT?"

As a young cadet, I learned from a seasoned non-commissioned officer (NCO) who served in Vietnam why I should treat people with dignity and respect. The command sergeant major (CSM) and the most senior enlisted rank (usually with 18-plus years of experience) called me into his ROTC office and asked, "What is the difference between a PFC [private first class] and a 2LT [second lieutenant]?" Seeing the perplexed look on my face, he looked me straight in the eye, and answered his own question: "The PFC has been promoted at least once . . . now remember that when you're a 2LT . . . that is all, cadet." I had no idea what he was talking about, but I left his office quickly to avoid other unanswerable questions.

His message was actually a simple one. Rank and experience aren't always the same. A PFC has the enlisted grade of E-3, which means they have been in the Army a short time and have some experience. By contrast, a 2LT has the officer grade of O-1, the very first rank in the officer corps. Most likely, though, the 2LT has little to no experience in the Army. So, the E-3 may have more experience and can provide a greater contribution.

His message was not to discount others on my team

because they are young or new. We need to empower everyone on our teams. We must see past the rank, treat people with dignity and respect, and understand they are valuable team members.

Rank and pay are often associated together, which is accurate. More accurately, though, rank is a sign of accountability due to experience and ability to anticipate events and consequences of decisions. Rank and pay are both earned.

As if he knew when I deciphered his message, that same CSM called me to his office shortly before I graduated from ROTC. He said he had another question for me. "Cadet Hinck, what is the difference between respect of rank, respect of position, and personal respect?" In his typical style, the CSM locked eyes with me and advised, "The first two are automatic, and the last one you get the old fashioned way... you earn it!"

I stood there staring back at him, his rank of CSM, and the many positions he held over the years, especially in Vietnam. He interrupted my deep thought: "Hinck, what are you staring at? Get out of my office."

NCOs truly are the backbone of our Army.

LESSON #9   Develop an attack mindset to win in any situation.

"Cadet, you have two options: Attack now or attack later."

I'm known for asking "what are my options" to all ranks, and

I have never been a fan of either/or situations. Ever been in an argument over where to go out for food? If the other person provides three or four options, then all parties win. In one particular situation, I was given only two options.

As a third-year cadet, I was evaluated on my ability to lead a small group of fellow cadets on a field training exercise (FTX) at Fort Ord near Monterey, California. My evaluator offered only two options: attack now or attack later. I felt I was back home with my father telling me I was going to church and could either like it or not. The lesson of having the right attitude gave me some confidence; however, this situation was more complex because it involved other people who were counting on me to pick the right option.

The challenge with this night mission was both options produced the same outcome: failure. The enemy force was larger, possessed more weapons, had vehicles for speed, and was comprised of senior cadets. They were bigger, faster, and better. If we attacked now, the enemy would overrun us or setup a speedy defense while they maneuvered to our flank and tore through our hasty fighting positions. If we attacked later, the enemy would quickly surround us and attack our limited defense whenever they chose. As a fan of the original Star Trek series, I was reminded of the Kobayashi Maru, a scenario in which Starfleet cadets face a no-win situation to test character and problem-solving skills.

In a no-win situation, how a person acts and reacts says much about their leadership skills. The lesson of my scenario was to make a decision and execute based on surprise, concentration, tempo, and audacity, which are the principles of offensive operations (*U.S. Army Field Manual* 3-0, 1 Nov 2001).[4] I decided to split my forces and attack immediately from two different directions without any reconnaissance. I called the next most experienced person, a new cadet who had prior service in the Army and in a few schools including the primary leadership development training. I skipped about three ranks to choose her experience and credibility. I needed someone who could think quickly, who others would follow, and who had great fitness and endurance. She would lead half the team, and I, the other half.

We would each move quickly but as quietly as possible on opposite directions for ten minutes about ¾ to one mile through the woods and some sparse trees. At the ten-minute mark, we would both turn toward the enemy and move deliberately closer into an attack position. The final movement would be on our stomachs to move as close as possible to the enemy vehicles. At the 20-minute mark, she would attack, followed 30 seconds later by my team's attack. The objective was to confuse the enemy, exploit the situation, and get to the heart of their formation to attack their command vehicle. Most of us would probably die (indicated by a buzzer going off on our gear). But in this scenario, most people would die.

Yet we had some advantages. They were faster, but we were more agile. They were bigger and would want to coordinate their actions, but we moved with independent freedom to maneuver. They had more weapons but would react to action off the first attack and not have time to adjust to our second attack. We had our reputations at stake. We were motivated. Our plan was simple and bold. It would be conducted with violent execution.

As we moved out, my evaluator whispered, "No one has ever done this before." I thought to myself, *Well, I've never done this before, and there's a first time for everything.* My thought was interrupted by my falling into a hole with a terrific sound of my equipment hitting the ground, and the spraining of my left ankle. For me, the exercise was over before the attack could begin. The evaluator yelled for a medic and radioed in the situation. When my second in charge returned to my location, I told her to attack. She immediately understood my intent of surprise and audacity. She moved quickly. When the evaluator asked what I told her, I simply replied while still in pain, "Attack!" He smiled, shook his head, but did not share our plan over the radio.

To say we got clobbered would be an understatement. The senior cadets figured out our strategy but not until two of my people closed within grenade range of their command vehicles. I learned more about leadership that day than any book can provide. I learned attack is a mindset. I learned to focus on what is possible under the circumstances, formulate an aggressive plan, then attack. It is this attack mentality that guided me throughout my career and positioned me to win in any situation. Attitude and decisions say much about character. Attack!

LESSON #10 Leadership means accomplishing a task to standard regardless of conditions.

"Gas! Gas! Gas!" Fighting in a Chemical Mask and Suit

Every Soldier learns that every task has a standard for successful accomplishment regardless of the conditions in which it is performed. For example, whether during daylight or nighttime conditions, a Soldier must accurately hit a target (the task) a specific number of times or within a time limit. And the Army trains in the toughest conditions. The most challenging conditions include working in darkness while wearing heavy equipment or a gas mask.

As a cadet, I remember going to the Fort Ord range. I completed my day and night weapon qualifications with high scores and was feeling proud. Our senior trainer, a master sergeant who trained with a ranger battalion, overheard my boasts. When I heard, "Cadet Hinck, post," I ran to the senior NCO and reported. He asked if I thought I was a good shot.

"Absolutely," I replied. The next three words will ring in my head forever.

"Gas! Gas! Gas!"

Those words indicate that chemicals, potentially deadly, have been released. The task is to don a gas mask, put on a chemical suit, and take a defensive posture against a possible assault. The standard time is within nine seconds for the gas mask and eight minutes for the full chemical suit. Because I trained repeatedly, I met all the time standards. Unfortunately, I was not prepared for the next two tasks.

I was instructed to do jumping jacks to get particles off my mask and suit. My weapon would remain in one hand, as it needed airing out as well. With my sweat pouring, the master sergeant commanded, "Hinck, follow me," as he jogged to the rifle range 400 meters down the road. Running in full chemical suit on a sunny California afternoon will test anyone's endurance. Exhausted, perspiration and salt stinging my eyes, the master sergeant reminded me about weapon safety and gave me a full magazine of rounds. Instructed to get into the prone position, I flopped to the ground only to be told to get back up and correctly take the prone position. (There are Army standards and then there are senior NCO standards.)

"Cadet Hinck, you have 40 rounds with which you will engage the target. On my command, you will have one minute to engage the target. Raise your left hand to indicate you understand your task." After acknowledging my instructions, I was given the preparatory command of "Firers, watch your lane," followed shortly by the command of execution, "Fire! Fire! Fire!"

Breathing hard, sweating profusely, and shaking from fear of failure, I struggled to see the target only 50 meters away. Although my weapon was pointed at the target, I had no idea where my first round landed . . . or my second . . . or my third.

"Cadet Hinck, remember the basics of breathing, sight picture, and trigger control." With 45 seconds remaining, I focused on controlling my exasperation and shaking. The next two rounds hit bottom left, a place I was not aiming. I adjusted high right, and the round hit high and right of the center. I re-aimed at the center, slowly pulled the trigger, and put one round just to the left of center, one near center, and another high right again. I heard the command, "Cease fire, cease fire, cease fire. Cadet Hinck, put your weapon on safe."

In sixty seconds, I fired nine rounds with only two coming close to center. I was beyond humbled. With the all-clear command, I took off my gas mask and watched sweat drip from the face cover. I was told to take a knee and drink water, but no other words were exchanged.

After about five minutes of eternity, the master sergeant instructed, "Get ready . . . Gas! Gas! Gas!" I redonned my mask and was instructed to resume the prone fighting position. Again, I was commanded to engage my target with 40 rounds in one minute.

My NCO leaned down and told me, "Being exhausted, sore, sweaty, uncomfortable, and frustrated are all conditions. Concentrate on the task at hand to hit your target."

This continued two more times until I successfully expended all 40 rounds in one minute. My best was to hit the target 32 times out of 40, a qualifying score. I learned a good shot depends on the conditions, and, more importantly, a leader accomplishes the task to standard regardless of the conditions.

Bosses do not want to hear why we are unable to accomplish a task. Most reasons are, at best, lame excuses. Although some are valid and legitimate, as leaders, we must find ways to get the job done right, on time, and within budget. We may have to continue trial and error until we surpass the standard despite tough conditions. Almost every reason is like a condition. Regardless of the conditions, leaders accomplish the task to standard.

LESSON #11 Self-confidence is needed to lead others.

"A312, you will stand in my door until you graduate."

Increasing confidence means overcoming fears. The Army has a method for this known as the direct method. Some jokingly call it "gaining confidence the old fashioned way" because it is earned, so to speak. I earned my confidence by overcoming my fear of heights at the U.S. Army Airborne School (Jump School) at Fort Benning, Georgia. I know it seems odd for an aviator to be afraid of heights, but some say the real fear is one of falling, not height itself. Whether it's being four or more stories high or falling from that height, I don't like it.

Naturally, I was selected to attend airborne school. The course was three weeks and consisted of Ground Week, Tower Week, and Jump Week. During day one of training, we were asked by a black hat (an NCO in charge) if anyone was afraid of heights. I was seasoned enough to know not to raise my hand and single myself out.

The first week of training was first-class. We were

conditioned from formation runs and exercises in a sawdust pit as well as taught the proper handling of gear, jumping fundamentals, and learning to properly execute a parachute landing fall (PLF), which was about transferring energy from the feet throughout the rest of the body to land without injury. I didn't have issues jumping from the lateral drift assembly or the 34-foot tower.

Week two focused on jumping from more towers in different conditions, understanding how to safely exit an aircraft, and learning to employ the reserve chute. The culmination was landing from a 250-foot tower. High winds prevented my entire class from jumping off the 250-foot tower, yet we moved onto the final week anyway. For me, this was a fine example of good lost opportunity.

Jump week entailed completing five jumps including some in varied formations, one night jump, one "Hollywood" jump with no gear, and one with full combat gear.

During each pass of the drop zone, one stick (or group) of jumpers exited each side of the aircraft, normally a C-130. The head of each stick stood in the door to wait until the jump light turned green, and the jumpmaster delivered a slap to the butt as the go ahead. I dreaded having to stand in the door, but I was in the middle of my stick, so it eased my worries. However, due to winds and weather and good old Murphy's Law, I ended up first in my chalk.

At that point, I was more confident in my equipment and training than I was of myself. I shuffled to the door, turned 90 degrees, and maintained a read-to-jump posture facing the exit door with my foot at the edge. The few seconds thinking about jumping were the longest stretch of time in my life. When the light turned green and the swat came, I did nothing. I remained in the ready-to-jump posture, slightly trembling. Within a second, the jumpmaster's boot was on my butt, kicking me out the door. The air filled my opened parachute with the expected force, jolting me.

The training immediately took over. My hands reached up to grab the risers, and I visually checked my canopy for problems. I scanned the horizon, ready to steer into the wind and away from other jumpers. Calmness overcame me as I drifted in a controlled fall for the next few seconds. My PLF was textbook, and I began to gather my chute to get to the rally point. On my way, I noticed a black hat with a megaphone yelling in my direction. I reported to the sergeant who told me to see the jumpmaster before my next jump, which I did upon returning to the rally point at Lawson Army Airfield.

He told me three things: "A312 [my designation], you are not afraid of heights. You don't have confidence in your equipment or the people the Army trained. And you will stand in my door until you graduate."

The senior NCO pulled me aside and whispered in my ear, "All Soldiers are expected to have confidence in their equipment and their training. As an officer, I expect you to have confidence in your Soldiers and yourself."

On next four jumps, I was first to the door. I was less fearful with each jump. My confidence rose to the same levels I had in my training, my equipment, and my black hats. My fear of heights was outmatched by my fear of not succeeding and, thus, disappointing my black hats.

Confidence is a product of trust in trainers, training, equipment, and the self. By the final jump, I was not over my fear, but I was able to control my fear and not let it prevent me from making the night jump in full combat gear. I graduated with my class and continued to Fort Bragg, North Carolina to join the 82nd Airborne Division, or so I thought.

CHAPTER 3

Entry-Level Leadership: Learning the Basics

LESSON #12 Appreciate life, take nothing for granted, and understand why everything is relative.

"I want you to draw the human eye."

Every military flight school has a rich history of legends based upon proven practices, unique traditions as well as a repetition of studying, simulators, table-talk, pre-flight, flight, and post-flight. The relationship between instructor pilot and student is built on trust. The student has immaculate trust that the instructor knows everything. The instructor has immeasurable trust that the student knows little to nothing. So, at Fort Rucker, home of Army aviation, it is the instructor's job to impart knowledge and skills of learning to fly and maintain control of a helicopter.

One of my instructors was Ms. Mary Boucher, who, at the time, we all thought must have been picked to fly God or the President (a testament to her skill and experience, not her age). When we met, she had been flying longer than I had been alive, and, as the joke goes, she had more cool down time than I had flight time. Like all the flight instructors, she was as tough as a woodpecker's lips. She was my primary instructor for the initial phase of the aeroscout track, the most academically challenging track. We studied several topics each class period and were asked questions in a group format. That was followed by an intensive session of the instructor grilling two students before heading for aircraft pre-flight.

On an unforgettable day in April 1992 during table-talk time, Ms. Boucher slid a blank sheet of paper to me and matter-of-factly stated, "I want you to draw the human eye." Understanding how the eye worked was part of the curriculum and important to understanding the physiological blind spot and night vision.

Our instructors had a good sense of when a student didn't know something. At that particular moment, I presented a double challenge for her. My lack of ability to draw the eye was compounded by having not studied it. I never thought I would actually have to draw the anatomy of an eye. I mentally questioned why I needed to know how to draw the cornea, iris, pupil, lens, sclera, retina, retinal wall, optic nerve, and so on. Over the next four weeks, she would slide the sheet of paper, waiting for my brilliance. And she had the patience of Job. After trial and error, I finally met her standard. I thought she was trying to make the course hard to live up to the reputation.

The time for my check ride came, which is done with a different instructor. I had a guest instructor, a senior instructor at Fort Rucker. After polite introductions, we sat down for table-talk. The first thing he did was slide a blank sheet of paper to me followed by the statement: "Draw the human eye."

I don't know if he or I was more amazed by my achievement of completing the task swiftly and with confidence. I had the best check ride that day. Not only because I performed well on the drawing, but also because I performed above standard on the required skills. My performance was honed by repetition of performing a task to Mary Boucher's standard, which was tougher than the school standard. I did well because Boucher ensured I had already exceeded the standard for every skill I would face that day. She gave me the skills to excel when the opportunity presented itself.

Anyone can acquire skills through persistence to achieve the standard in the toughest of conditions. To this day, I define luck as the point at which skill and opportunity meet. Luck is success which has been built with hard work and persistence. However, what looks like luck to the casual observer is really success driven by hard work and persistence. The casual observer doesn't see the time and energy put forth to achieve the skill. Whether it appears as luck or success, the skills to accomplish the task to standard always exists. And whenever there's a standard, I bump it up to the Mary Boucher level.

LESSON #13   Know the audience before speaking.

"You're NOT John Taylor," and "Do you live in a barn?"

One fundamental of effective communication is knowing the

audience. The methods of understanding audience include observation, research, questioning, and working with them. Similarly, the reason the Army teaches Soldiers to conduct reconnaissance to gain valuable decision-making information is for leaders to know with whom they are speaking before they open their mouths. Knowing the audience is a major component of intelligent preparation before a job interview, before joining an organization, and before having a lunch meeting with prospective clients. Not knowing the audience prevents the message from being understood or other unintended consequences.

Not knowing my audience on a late evening and a cold morning at Fort Bragg ended with unexpected results. After 16 months of officer and survival training as well as flight, air assault, and airborne schools, I arrived to Fort Bragg as a second lieutenant, ready for the world.

On the first Friday night after arriving, some of the other lieutenants and I decided to hit the officer's club. After a few drinks, my courage was skyrocketing. I noticed two women trying to get a drink. I offered to assist. I told one of the women, "Nice shoes." When she looked down, I asked the bartender to get them a drink. He replied they wanted strawberry daiquiris, and he was waiting for more mix.

I took the opportunity and said, "Well, I am John Taylor, and my father, General Taylor, the Corps Chief of Staff, and I would greatly appreciate you not making these ladies wait much longer. Let me buy them a drink."

One of the women chuckled and said, "Thank you, we would appreciate the drink, but you're not John Taylor."

I responded, "Oh, why do you say that?"

What she said will forever remind me to know my audience. She offered, "Well, I am Jen Taylor, my father is General Taylor, and I don't have a brother."

What were the chances I would use that made-up line on one of the few people who could call me out? My nervous, surprised laughter was matched by almost hysterical laughter of both women and the bartender. Weeks later, upon first meeting General Taylor, he looked at me and said, "Ah, John, the son I never had."

I learned the importance of knowing my audience again on my first day of physical fitness with my aerial scout platoon and attack helicopter company on a Monday morning. I lived off post and arrived early for physical training (PT). Fort Bragg is chilly in November, so I went to the barracks until PT started. I saw some Soldiers entering the barracks to wait in a common area, so I followed them in. The door, hampered by a broken hinge, did not close behind me. Not noticing the door was still open, I continued inside the room.

I was abruptly stopped when a voice joked, "Hey, do you live in a barn?" I turned my head to see an older man, evidenced by his light grey hair and weathered face, sitting relaxed in a chair while scolding me. The open door and his comment halted the conversation and drew all attention to me.

As a young buck officer, I immediately told him, "No, what is your problem?" To say he didn't care would be an understatement. He had a give-a-shit-factor of zero. So, I ordered, "I am Lieutenant Hinck. Why don't you close the door yourself?" That statement got him up, but not for the reasons I thought.

He said, "I didn't open the door, sir." The room of about a dozen people was fully quiet, the atmosphere, awkward and tense.

I replied, "You're right. Why don't you go to the position of parade rest while I shut the door?" The Soldier did as I requested. I slowly and purposefully closed the door. By now, it was time for PT, but no one was moving. With my words, "You're dismissed," the man moved out of the barracks to the PT field. The other Soldiers followed out of the barracks. I fell in with my company formation.

After stretching, pushups, and sit-ups, the formation went for a run. Part way through, a young Soldier ran to our formation and asked "Where is Lieutenant Hinck?"

Startled, I said, "Here."

The Soldier stoically said, "Sir, please follow me. The battalion commander wants to see you in his office."

The battalion commander was a lieutenant colonel, four ranks above mine, and had been in the Army for 18 years compared to my 14 months. I reported to his office at the position of attention. He told me to go to parade rest, and then asked, "Lieutenant, why did you have to get in a pissing match with my command sergeant major?"

I replied, "Sir, I've never met the CSM."

He looked at me, "He was the guy you admonished in the barracks in front of other Soldiers."

I vividly remember what the commander said as an oh-crap look spread over my face: "But besides that, why did I have to listen to the Corps Chief of Staff asking me about why you are impersonating a son he doesn't have? John, you've been at Bragg less than a week, and you're already on the radar of a general officer, Soldiers are talking about you, and you and my Sergeant Major were squaring off in the barracks. The good news is that you have a few years to understand the importance of knowing who you are talking to before you open your mouth. I recommend you visit the CSM to iron out your relationship, and just be yourself when you're trying to pick up young ladies in the officer club. That is all."

I moved out hurriedly and with humility.

LESSON #14   Seeing things is different from
                  understanding them.

"Tell me what you see in the motor pool."

We can look at something and not understand what we are seeing. How we comprehend what we see is colored by our experiences, perspectives, and associated values. A new employee versus a CEO will see things differently because of their levels of experience. A salesperson and a budget analyst will view managing resources differently because of their perspectives. Someone who drives to work up against someone who walks to work will place different value on a weather forecast.

Every Thursday at Fort Bragg, most units conducted

motor stables to focus on vehicle and equipment readiness. Someone new to the Army who has not worked around vehicles would see a motor pool in a different manner from a seasoned Soldier. On my first trip to our unit motor pool, my platoon sergeant (PSG), a sergeant first class with ten to twelve years of experience, said he wanted to make sure I understood what to look for in the motor pool in case I was asked by the company commander or battalion commander. Also, as a platoon leader, I was responsible for aircraft and vehicle maintenance.

My PSG asked this simple question, "Tell me what you see in the motor pool?" Before I could answer, he offered that I probably saw vehicles lined up with Soldiers working on them. Not knowing where the conversation was going, I nodded. He continued in his easy southern drawl, "LT, you need to understand what to look for so you understand what you see. You see the vehicles, but do you also see the drip pans under each vehicle to catch any leaks, and the chock blocks at the back left tire, so the vehicle remains in place? You see Soldiers working on vehicles, but do you also see the operating manuals open as they conduct operator-level work? You see the vehicles lined up, but do you understand that it is done to ensure attention to detail and uniformity? You see vehicles being backed up, but do you see the ground guide in a position to clear the vehicle as well as remain out of the vehicle path as precaution for safety?"

His explanations opened my eyes. He concluded, "LT, seeing things is different than understanding what you see. You need to see our flight line with that same understanding 'cause I don't think you need any more office calls with the battalion commander." He smiled at me. What a funny NCO.

LESSON #15 Why your boss wants situational understanding AND recommendations.

What? So What? Now What?

Much has been written about the importance of leaders understanding what they see and hear to make a decision. Effective leaders go beyond the facts of a situation. A boss wants and expects employees to understand why facts are important, then what to do with those facts. While several hierarchies of information explain knowledge, one breaks it down to data, information, knowledge and wisdom or DIKW.[1] Data is stuff without meaning like letters or symbols. Information is formed when meaning is placed on the data. Knowledge is information that has value. And Wisdom is knowing what to do or not to do with knowledge.

The DIKW model explains how people think or know something in a graduated manner. However, the model does not explain how knowledge is applied or how wisdom is used. Because leaders must think *and* act, two parts must be added to provide framework for applying knowledge and wisdom: situational understanding and decision-making.

Situational understanding is applying knowledge to a situation. During a specific event, a leader will place value on information that is relevant to that situation. Furthermore, decision-making is moving from comprehending the situation to making a situation-specific change. Three basic questions provide an easy framework for situational understanding and decision-making: **What? So What? Now What?**[2]

The **What** answers with facts to describe what is happening, and facts provide meaning and details. The **So What** assigns value to the facts. The **Now What** either recommends a course of action or a decision. In essence, the leader moves from a position of "know what" to "now what" only by knowing what to do with the situation-specific knowledge. The **Now What** is a future-oriented action, which should improve the situation.

My IPs (Instructor Pilots) used the format when teaching pilots to react to emergency procedures. We would discuss the facts, what the facts meant to us pilots, and then what actions would remedy the situation. In training, many of these discussions preceded the actual manipulation of any flight controls to simulate an emergency condition.

One of my commanders in the Apache community used the format in teaching tactics, especially offensive aerial tactics within the "action-reaction-counteraction" process of battle. Each action caused a reaction, which was followed by a counteraction. During each step, he asked **What? So What? Now What?** to ensure we could clearly identify the facts, apply those facts, know the possible solutions, and, most importantly, decide on the best course of action.

I applied the model in several situations throughout my career. During the conflict in the Balkans, specifically involving the buildup of U.S. forces in Albania in preparation for offensive operations in Macedonia, I was the logistics officer for an Attack Helicopter Regiment of 48 Apaches. The water-soaked ground needed reinforcement to hold 20,000-pound Apaches. As part of a small force which went forward to assess conditions in Albania, I was on a team which had to make a rapid decision to halt aircraft in Italy because the ground had to be built-up to hold the weight of the 20,000 pound aircraft. Because the water table was roughly a foot below the ground level, the ground was extremely muddy and needed reinforcement with gravel and steel plates. Delaying the aircraft would delay the timeline to train and prepare for missions, yet we needed time to properly prepare landing conditions for the aircraft. Only by understanding the **What? So What? Now What?** of the situation could the right decision be made with wisdom.

In Afghanistan during Operation Enduring Freedom, I commanded Task Force ODIN-Afghanistan, a special aviation unit of 43 fixed wing and unmanned systems and 740 plus Soldiers and civilians. One of unmanned systems was the Warrior Alpha, a remote-controlled aircraft which could fire Hellfire missiles and had an advanced camera/imaging system. During combat operations, leaders make decisions based on the information immediately available with a clear realization that every decision has consequences. On one particular early morning, one of my crews flying the Warrior-Alpha found insurgents planting an IED on a road. While the actions were clearly hostile intent, we had to get clearance from the ground commander and ensure now friendly troops were in the immediate area in order to prevent fratricide. Although the process took a matter of minutes, by the time we had approval, the insurgents had moved away from the road and to a small house. At the time, the rules of engagement did not allow us to fire on a house if we did not know it was absolutely clear of civilians. The purpose was to prevent unnecessary collateral damage. We had a bad guy in our sights, and many wanted us to fire, but I made the decision not to engage based on my understanding of the situation. The **So What?** and **Now What?** became key questions in my decision not to fire our weapon system. Later, we found out there were other civilians, including children, in the small house. The decision not to engage was a tough one but the best decision under the circumstances.

The three questions remain with me because of their simplicity. They work for any level in any situation. Good leaders must arm themselves with effective methods to understand the situation and make the right decision.

LESSON #16 People support what they help create.

"You're in charge of the Battalion Organizational Day."

I joined my first Army unit as a second lieutenant in 3rd Battalion, 229th Aviation Regiment at Fort Bragg. The battalion commander called me into his office: "LT Hinck, you're in charge of the Battalion Organizational Day . . . make it better than last year." A long-held tradition in most military forces for the newest or most junior ranks is being assigned mundane tasks. It's a rite of passage. As I left head-quarters, I considered to whom I should speak regarding last year's event. I spoke with Soldiers of all ranks across the battalion as well as family members. Three recurring themes emerged: family-focused, fun for everyone, and a location that encouraged high attendance.

These goals seemed reasonable, but I wanted more information. I revisited the people I spoke with and asked what would be fun for their families and ideas for great loca-tions. Most people wanted a range of activities like events for kids and spouses, athletic competitions, or a chili cook-off. Some suggested community involvement like the local fire department spraying water from the truck. Others recom-mended holding the event at a lake for fun and relaxation on the late spring day.

I also learned the previous year was planned by only two officers without representation from other units and ranks. This last piece of information became critical in how I would approach planning, preparation, and execution of the upcoming Battalion Organizational Day. I wanted it to be an all-encompassing unit and family event. I received backing from battalion leadership to form a planning group comprised of representatives from each unit and our family readiness groups. We looked at several locations but settled on a site near Simmons Lake, close to Simmons Airfield on Fort Bragg.

Our event was the best-attended and longest-lasting

Organizational Day in our unit's history. I applied the principle of "people support what they help create," one the Order of DeMolay taught me. I asked people what they wanted, formed a guiding coalition, and delivered. The Soldiers and families were part of the process from the beginning and truly felt part of the development.

LESSON #17 Leaders train two levels down and understand two levels up.

Knowing Subordinates' Subordinates and Your Bosses' Bosses

The Army produces a wealth of material that captures concepts, lessons, tactics, procedures, and principles regarding the what, why, and how the Army does business. The information is arranged in a cascading layout, beginning with a macro view followed by detailed analysis specific to the fields of expertise such as infantry, aviation, command, logistics, and so on. This knowledge is categorized in Army doctrine publications (ADPs), Army doctrine reference publications (ADRPs), field manuals (FMs), Army techniques publications (ATPs), and digital applications (APPs). There are numbers that follow each name, which relate to levels of command, branch, function, or specialty. Common themes in these publications are leader responsibilities and training fundamentals.

Good leaders knowing their subordinates' subordinates

and having a solid understanding of their bosses' bosses are codified in Army publications, specifically dealing with doctrine, operations process, leadership, and training units. Recurring themes "to know and train subordinates at least two levels down" and "fully understand the commander's intent two levels up" are found in more than one issue of Army manuals.[3] Covering this content in multiple publications facilitates shared understanding of what's happening in the organization laterally and horizontally. It provides a clear link between direct leadership and organizational leadership.

Additionally, the themes are formalized in the Army's evaluation process using officer evaluation reports (OERs) and the method to communicate operations orders (OPORDs). Every officer completes an OER support form, which includes objectives to achieve based on assigned position and an understanding of the objectives of the supervisor (the boss) and senior rater (the boss's boss). The OPORD format is used for training, war plans, and combat situations.

In one ADRP[4], the commander's intent and concept of the operation portions in the OPORD explain the purposes and tasks required to achieve the end state (future conditions). These are linked to the higher command missions and explain the what and why of the mission. The concept of the operation explains the how and is nested with the higher command missions.

The above principles are ingrained in every military leader, but sometimes, it takes both a mentor and constant application to firmly cement the principles into a leader's foundation. A platoon leader is expected to train his squads and teams as well as understand the mission of his company and battalion. My company commander was constantly training me to perform at the next level, so he expected me to know what the entire company (including the attack and scout platoons, support assets, and battalion and brigade missions) was expected to do. His emphasis on the principles to train two levels down and understand two levels up provided a foundation that served me well in future positions.

As the assistant battalion operations officer at Fort Bragg, I wrote the OPORDs for field training exercises and aerial gunnery events. As the brigade plans officer in South Korea, I wrote the aviation war plans and had to grasp how aviation assets were incorporated from battalion to theater level (six levels above the battalion). As the brigade logistics officer in Germany, Bosnia, and Albania, it was critical to know how supply and movements occurred laterally and horizontally. As the battalion executive officer in Afghanistan, I needed to know the breadth of missions performed by our sections and the requirements from adjacent units and higher commands. As the battalion operations officer in South Korea, it was my responsibility to know how the aviation assets set conditions for other forces and how aviation was nested across the entire peninsula. As the battalion commander at Fort Hood, I trained two levels down and understood as much as three levels up to build an aviation task force for successful operations in Afghanistan.

In every regard, the principle to know and train two levels down and understand two levels up echoed across assignments. Effective leaders should know their subordinates' subordinates and understand of the mission of their bosses' bosses; it is the only way to see the big picture to solve big problems.

LESSON #18   Business is business; make the bottom line.

Orangutan Orange and Kneepads

A Dining Out is a semi-formal event attended by Soldiers and spouses where subordinate units sit together, enjoy a catered meal, partake in celebratory toasts and a grog bowl ceremony, and perform comedy skits. Also, a junior officer is selected to act as Mr. Vice, a role subordinate only to the ranking officer of the mess, usually the unit commander. As the junior commissioned officer, I was selected to help put on the skit for my company and as Mr. Vice. I took both roles seriously, wanting to make the event memorable.

Following the grog bowl ceremony—in which unit representatives pour a bunch of liquids (alcohol, non-alcohol, Tabasco, etc.) into an oversized punch bowl—Mr. Vice is instructed to test if the grog is even consumable by drinking the heavily alcoholic brew. In keeping with tradition, I dipped my cup into the grog, took one swallow, looked at the senior officer, and said, "Due to my inexperience, I am not sure I can determine if this fine brew is truly fit for human consumption, but perhaps an officer of your wise nature could make this important decision." Realizing I brashly challenged the battalion commander, the room hushed and focused on the head table.

The battalion commander stood up and pointed at me, "Lieutenant Hinck, bring me a cup!"

Expecting this, I hid a large beer stein under the grog bowl table. I grabbed the stein, dipped it in the grog, filled it, and looked back at the head table, "Roger, moving!"

All eyes were on me as I proceeded to the head table. I slammed the stein on the table in front of my senior commander, keeping my eyes fixed on him. Without a word, he stood, grabbed the stein, drank the contents, and slammed the stein down. The room erupted in applause, but he kept his intense gaze on me. The room quieted.

He barked, "LT, the grog is fit for you to drink from it... now go back with this same stein and follow my previous order." I did not expect this order. I weighed about 150 pounds and had not eaten much during the ceremony. Yet, how could I back down? Of course, I complied and downed the stein of grog. While everyone applauded, my battalion commander stared at me with mild disappointment.

My brashness of breaking with tradition to challenge a senior officer could have been overcome if not for my performance during my unit's skit. A fellow officer and I represented our company with a tribute to Johnny Carson's Carnac the Magnificent. My fellow lieutenant played Carnac, and I played Ed McMahon. For those unfamiliar, Carnac was like a swami who wore large, sparkling turban, held envelopes containing questions to his forehead, announced the answer to each question, then opened the envelope to read the question, which was the joke's punchline.

For our skit, the first few envelopes were somewhat harmless but funny enough to warm up the crowd. When the sixth envelope was held up, Carnac (my buddy in crime), announced, "Orangutan Orange."

As Ed McMahon would do, I repeated the phrase, "Orangutan Orange."

The envelope was opened to reveal the question, "What is the current color of the battalion commander's hair?"

The room erupted in laughter knowing the battalion commander's hair turned different colors thanks to a special conditioner he used to control a scalp ailment. His wife was roaring, slapping the table. The battalion commander was stone silent with a fixed gaze on us.

Nervously, we proceeded to our seventh and, unexpectedly, last envelope. Holding it up, Carnac stated, "Kneepads."

I echoed, "Kneepads."

With a tearing of the envelope, the question is revealed, "What does Lieutenant Smith wear when he goes to see the battalion commander?"

The response was nervous laughter and quizzical looks. No one at the head table laughed. The battalion commander stood and declared, "Your skit is complete. Bring up the next company for their skit."

Immediately after the ceremony, I was called in to speak privately with my company commander and the battalion commander for a one-way conversation. The words were something along the lines of, "John, you are a fine officer, bold, brash, even funny, but tonight, you crossed the

line. I don't mind you breaking tradition of the grog ceremony . . . that was entertaining. And although I don't like you
making fun of my scalp condition, it was an easy poke, and
I can laugh at myself. But when you humiliate a fellow
officer and demean his character, you cross the line. You
singled out Lieutenant Smith and a professional relationship
I have with one of my junior officers. By making him the butt
of your joke, you made the skit a personal attack on his character, which is uncalled for and simply not professional. Business is business, and in our job, we make decisions based on
being professional, not personal. You are his junior, and you
must know your limits . . . If you go beyond your limits or
make something personal, then, by definition, you are not a
professional. Many people thought what you did was funny,
and you certainly will be talked about for the skit, but know
that you have some ground to make up with me now."

Some lessons make such an impact that the point lasts
forever. Needless to say, I remembered the lesson that if we
go beyond our professional limits or make something
personal, then, by definition, we are not professional. Hence,
I strived to remain an honorable, professional leader.

LESSON #19 Action completed is more
important than action pending.

"I want 'ed' words, not 'ing' ones!"

Due to the restructuring of Army aviation in 1994, my unit
at Fort Bragg transformed to a pure fleet of 24 AH-64

Apaches from a mixed organization of 18 AH-64 Apaches, 12 OH-58 Scout aircraft, and 3 UH-60 Blackhawks. During the transition, all 12 OH-58s were consolidated under one company, and I was given temporary command of them, called Team Scout. For a few months, I reported to a company commander—a West Point graduate with ratings in the AH-64, OH-58, and UH-60—who had a reputation for tactical excellence and intense leadership.

Shortly after hearing about my new position, my new boss, Captain Long, asked for an update on maintenance, training, and operations on Team Scout's 12 aircraft and 42 personnel. As I completed the first portion of my update, Captain Long asked, "John, when will your team complete the final maintenance inspections on all of your scout aircraft to prepare them for transfer?"

I replied, "Sir, we are working that issue, and I am confident my team will get the job done."

He said nothing in response, but, instead, asked another question: "John, when will you have completed all of the requirements for personnel moves as your people transition out of the unit?"

I replied, "Sir, we are working with the battalion personnel staff on that issue and have a plan in place."

Captain Long sternly replied, "John, I want 'ed' words, not 'ing' ones! When you say you are working or completing or maintaining, your actions are future oriented, which is fine if you have specific dates for completing tasks to standard. But your briefing is somewhat non-specific with a lack of the necessary details. So, I want you to start either providing me the details of your future-oriented action, or start using 'ed' words like solved, completed, achieved, which connote action passed. Action completed is more important than action pending completion or working."

The lesson remained with me so much that my own subordinates, in every unit thereafter, clearly understood the difference between "ing" words and "ed" words.

LESSON #20 How to exceed expectations and make a lasting impression.

Lollipops in the FARRP

The Army training and operations arenas work on a system of tasks, conditions, and standards. Regardless of the conditions, a Soldier and unit must perform specified tasks to a measurable standard. For every conceivable mission, the Army identified tasks at multiple levels individuals and organizations must perform to achieve a mission.

As platoon leader for the support platoon, assigned to Headquarters and Headquarters Company, 3rd Battalion, 229th Attack Helicopter Regiment, I led the unit of 33 soldiers and 17 vehicles to perform the tasks to safely refuel and rearm all 24 AH-64 Apache Helicopters. My company commander challenged me to make the forward area refueling and rearming point (FARRP) experience memorable for the pilots. Having no idea what he meant, I proceeded to find out from other pilots and my Soldiers how we could achieve my commander's vision.

Most of the time spent sitting in the aircraft at a refueling/rearming pad, pilots are focused on refueling procedures or taking a break from constantly being on the controls. It can be boring. As a pilot-in-command of OH-58 Scout aircraft, I often flew into the FARRP, so I saw the platoon's actions up close. In the previous two years as a scout platoon leader and pilot, no one ever talked to me while waiting in the FARRP. So, I made it a point to talk to as many pilots as possible. I wanted to talk with pilots to understand challenges and perceptions during FARRP operations.

For most individuals, improvements usually focus on their value to a company or how the company values them. Job performance centers on doing the right tasks the right way in a safe, suitable work environment. Their worth is associated with how they feel about peers, subordinates, superiors, the organization, and themselves. The company pays employees to show value, rewarding good job performance and celebrating wins. This made my questions simple, "How's your training going? Any mission updates from what you've seen? How are my Soldiers doing? Is there anything we can do to make your FARRP experience better?" The answers were generally positive, and all appreciated my inquiries. Yet, I didn't feel we were creating a memorable experience.

In talking with my platoon sergeant, a sergeant first class with over 14 years in the Army and three small children, he said pilots are like kids; they like a token of thanks.

Inquisitively, I prompted my NCO, "What do you mean give them a token?"

His reply was memorable: "Sir, it doesn't really matter what you give them as much as the simple gesture of you giving them something . . . kids like lollipops, so try giving the pilots a lollipop."

I chuckled, "Sergeant, although I think you're kidding me, I'll try the idea."

The next time we set up our FARRP, I brought a few bags of Tootsie Roll lollipops. We ran out before the end of the two-day operation. The pilots absolutely loved it. It gave them something to look forward to and briefly took their minds off of the mission. The pilots talked about the gesture at the hangar, in their offices, and among fellow pilots. On top of having the best record in safety and surpassing standards in rearming and refueling operations, my Soldiers received the most praise from pilots, elevating our status. The lollipops were a great lesson in doing small things for people to exceed expectations and make a lasting impression.

LESSON #21 Compare your performance to standards, not others.

Outrunning the Bear

The Army's slogan "Be All You Can Be" proved a great campaign in motivating many to join the ranks of our nation's finest. I was no exception. I joined the Army because of my family's history of service, my service in an honorable profession, my leadership development, and my desire to fly helicopters. I reveled in the Army's competitive spirit. During physical training, in the classroom, on the flight line, I wanted to be the best at what I did.

As a junior captain, I worked as the assistant operations officer to a major who was the battalion operations officer, the third in rank after the battalion commander and executive officer. In a brief with the major, we discussed his leader philosophy, training plan, performance objectives, and other expectations. He ended our first discussion with a hypothetical question, "If you and a friend are running from a bear, do you need to outrun the bear or just your friend?"

I joked, "Well, of course, my friend . . . if the objective is too not get caught by the bear."

My new boss's response felt like the wisdom of an ancient sage. "John, you need outrun the bear because, someday, your friend could be faster than you. Always compare your performance to the highest standard. In this case, it's the bear, not other people. Standards should remain constant unless you raise them. You have no control over others and their standards."

Outrunning the bear became a phrase I used throughout my career, conditioning myself and my team to achieve standards in the most challenging conditions. This lesson was the basis for how I trained my Apache Helicopter Company in Germany and won Top Gun Troop for two consecutive years.

LESSON #22 Punishment must fit the crime and the individual.

"I can take your wallet and your rank, but not your self-respect."

All U.S. Army personnel are governed by the Uniformed Code of Military Justice (UCMJ), which sets U.S. military law. In circumstances where service members commit lesser crimes, they can choose non-judicial punishments administered by a commanding officer or proceed to trial by court martial.[5] The maximum non-judicial punishments are lesser, and the commander decides based on evidence and witnesses. All NCOs and officers know the UCMJ. We review cases to understand situations we may face when leading Soldiers and, ultimately, responsibly upholding the UCMJ.

My first lesson in administering the correct punishment came as a platoon leader during non-judicial punishment of one of my Soldiers by our company commander. Specialist Jones was an outstanding Soldier, but he came from a tough home, had an anger problem and, when drinking, demeaned others. At work, he was one of our best aircraft crew chiefs and almost always did work better and faster than others. Yet, his anger and drinking got him into fights in the barracks and led him to say things that violated Army policy. His actions were well beneath that of a model Soldier. He was charged with disorderly conduct, disrespect to an NCO, and public intoxication. Evidence of his conduct included sworn statements by several witnesses, statements from the Military

Police, and Breathalyzer and lab results showing intoxication well above the legal limit. The Soldier admitted guilt and chose non-judicial punishment by our company commander.

During the punishment phase, a Soldier's leadership chain accompanies him to the commander's office. Hence, his squad leader, platoon sergeant, company first sergeant, and I, his platoon leader, were all in the room. In most proceedings, the accused Soldier is asked to state the maximum possible punishment. In this circumstance, after the Soldier stated the maximum punishment, the commander did something out of the ordinary.

He instructed the Soldier, who was standing at attention in front of his desk, to remove his uniform top, fold it, and place on the desk with the rank facing up. Next, he told the Soldier to remove his wallet and place it on the desk. Finally, he asked the Soldier to give him his self-respect. Specialist Jones looked puzzled. The room was quiet. No one said a word. The silent exchange between my Soldier and our company commander was broken when Specialist Jones started to look down. Our company commander said, "Specialist Jones, look at me . . . I can take your rank. And I can take your pay. But I can't take your self-respect, so why are you giving it away by your actions?"

Jones teared up. The captain said, "I know you can do better." Jones started crying, and our commander said in a fatherly way, "It's OK; let it out." It lasted a few minutes, but everyone remained standing. When Specialist Jones was done, he straightened up to the position of attention. The commander told him to recover his top and wallet. When

Jones was back in full uniform, our company commander said, "Before I dismiss you, I want you to complete an anger management program and finish an alcohol abuse program. I will give you the minimum punishments, but suspend all of them. You are one of my best Soldiers, and I expect you remain that way and always keep your self-respect. You are dismissed." Specialist Jones became our best Soldier and eventually rose through the NCO ranks as a model to others.

As military leaders, we must enforce good order and discipline and uphold the UCMJ. But more importantly, we must know our Soldiers and apply the whole-person concept when administering the UCMJ. In the end, we want to prevent the crime and rehab the person. To do so, punishment must fit the crime and the individual.

LESSON #23 Leaders set the standard by example... Do something half-assed or not at all sets a new standard.

Attending and Leading Unit Physical Training

Because I grew up in the Army ROTC program at California State University, Fresno, I was conditioned that officers attend and conduct PT with Soldiers. As a junior ROTC cadet, I had to attend physical training four days a week. As a senior cadet, I was expected to lead PT. As a platoon leader in my first aviation unit, I always attended PT with my

Soldiers. Even if I was flying at night, I would do PT with the night crew chiefs and other pilots.

During one PT session, the company commander, who was flying at night, showed up. The problem was my fellow platoon leader and some of his Soldiers, all on a night schedule, did not show up. Our company commander pulled me aside and asked if I knew why Lieutenant White and some of his personnel were not present. Although I did not know, I called his phone and left a message. We proceeded with the session, showered, ate breakfast, and returned to work.

Back at the hangar, our company commander called Lieutenant White and me into his office. No questions were asked. The commander looked at White and said, "Leaders set the standard by example . . . If you do something half-assed or not at all, you just set a new standard. Your Soldiers are watching you all the time. You will follow my example, and they will follow yours. Sweating with your Soldiers is paramount. For the next 90 days, you will lead all company physical training." We were both excused. I secretly thanked my ROTC cadre for instilling the lesson that leaders set the example, a lesson my fellow platoon leader experienced for the next 90 days.

LESSON #24 Why using checklists and
leader inspections matter.

"OK LT, now go ahead, and move your aircraft."

As part of the XVIII Airborne Corps, my aviation unit was

required to conduct worldwide contingency operations. Within hours of an alert notification, all unit personnel would ready themselves and the unit equipment, including vehicles and aircraft, for possible deployment via air, sea, or ground. Much of our equipment was already prepared for rapid movement. A few times each year, we conducted alert and training exercises to test our preparations and ability to meet corps' readiness standards. The Army established pre-combat checks (PCC) to check equipment against unit standards.

All units in the corps rehearse to meet the readiness and deployment requirements. So, on a Thursday at 4:18 a.m., my unit was alerted to conduct a no-notice readiness deployment exercise. The corps staff would inspect our readiness. Our battalion met the alert timelines; passed all equipment pre-packaging inspections; loaded four AH-64 Apaches, one UH-60 Blackhawk, and two OH-58s Kiowa Scouts (my aircraft) on two Air Force transport aircraft without error; and deployed to a local airfield. After the U.S.A.F. aircraft landed at an airfield about one hour away, the exercise was terminated. We surpassed every standard.

Following a debriefing by the evaluators, my battalion commander huddled the key leaders and said we would off-load our aircraft, and then fly back to Simmons Airfield. He then turned to me, "OK, LT, now go ahead and move your aircraft." I turned white. We had never off-loaded aircraft before. We kept our helicopters loaded on the Air Force aircraft and returned to Pope Air Force Base, where we would off-load and fly back to Simmons. My aircraft had skids, which required special handling gear with wheels to move them. The gear was required as part of the PCCs, but we always left them at Pope because we always off-loaded there.

I had just learned why using checklists and leader inspections matter. After that, the special handling gear always remained with the aircraft in case they had to be moved.

CHAPTER 4

Mid-Level Leadership: Practicing Standards of Excellence

LESSON #25 A team is only as great
as its weakest player.

The Undefeated Ultimate Frisbee Team

In officer continuing education, the Army sends all captains to a six-month advanced course designed to enhance technical and tactical skills. Every branch in the Army conducts a uniquely tailored program for officers within each branch. Some officers are selected to attend another branch's course. I wanted to return to where I began my flying career, so I attended the aviation officer advanced course at Fort Rucker in southern Alabama.

During my course, officers were organized into cohorts consisting of about 12 officers, mostly aviators with officers from other branches. It was a great experience to learn with fellow officers, exchange viewpoints about our profession, and sweat with them on the sports fields. One fellow aviator was an ultimate Frisbee fanatic. During our initial group meeting, he expressed only one interest: to head up sports, specifically our ultimate Frisbee team.

When we began practicing, he had one rule, "Everyone

plays." My team noticed other cohorts played only their strongest players, usually the bigger or faster male officers. The problem was those players would tire faster on the soccer-sized field. When the lesser capable players substituted into the game, their team's performance suffered.

My staff group practiced like we played. Our Frisbee coach taught everyone on our team to throw short, throw long, catch, and defend. Everyone learned. Everyone played. No other team could compete. We were the first and remain the only undefeated Ultimate Frisbee team at Fort Rucker. Our fellow officer raised our standards of excellence. On the Frisbee fields at Fort Rucker, I learned a team is only as great as the weakest player.

LESSON #26 Leaders know how to work hard, play hard, and rest hard.

My IV and "I've never seen that before!"

It was November in South Korea, and I didn't feel well. But as the plans officer for the aviation brigade assigned to 2nd Infantry Division, I powered through the sickness. Our unit, like most on the peninsula, was involved in an annual exercise called Foal Eagle, a Korean-U.S. forces joint event involving operations conducted from field sites, simulation centers, and from Navy platforms. As stated explained on Wikipedia[1]:

Foal Eagle 1998 was notable for a number of accomplishments. It marked the use of the Multiple Integrated Laser Engagement System (MILES) by all exercise participants, allowing forces to engage in realistic battle conditions without the loss of personnel or equipment. FE 98 marked the first time that the U.S. Navy established anti-submarine operations centers off both coasts of Korea with the U.S. Seventh Fleet's battle force, Task Force 70, in tactical command of ROK and American submarines. Foal Eagle 1998 also featured an amphibious assault involving seven battalions of ROK and U.S. forces.

I was the main planner for aviation and attack operations for the aviation brigade and felt I was somewhat indispensable. Besides, we got to wear MILES (Multiple Integrated Laser Engagement System) gear, which was cool because the technology allowed for more realistic war conditions. Despite being sick from a cold and tired from a lack of rest, I soldiered on until we redeployed to Camp Stanley, near Uijeongbu just north of Seoul. I reported to the flight surgeon, who, after finding out I lost seven pounds in two weeks and had a temperature of 104, gave me an IV to immediately help restore balance to my body and prevent any increase in temperature. This was a great idea, but I hate needles. The thought of having a needle in me for any length of time only made my condition worse.

The young medic was instructed to start the IV, and the doctor would return to check on me. With my head turned away, I felt the alcohol swab and tensed as the needle went into my arm. With the IV in progress, the medic turned his attention to another task. Something didn't feel right. I looked down, and I saw a growing bump near my vein where the needle was. I told the medic I wasn't feeling well. The medic returned to me and excitedly said, "Well, I've never seen that before!"

It was his reaction that caused the doctor to come running back. The doctor removed the needle and had me lie down. Apparently, the needle went through my vein, and the IV fluid was pooling just below my skin, creating a growing bulge. The technical term is a "blown vein," which normally causes swelling. Instead of getting an IV to rehydrate me, the doctor gave me a gallon of water to drink and five days of mandatory rest. I literally worked myself to exhaustion with a nearly catastrophic body temperature. I missed the next five days of work until my temperature returned to normal, and I was fully rehydrated.

I used to say, "Work Hard! Play Hard!" It was during my first tour in South Korea that I learned the lesson that changed it to, "Work hard, play hard, and rest hard!"

LESSON #27 Surround yourself with people of value because your reputation is at stake.

The Homily at Our Lady of Loreto

During deployments and far from home, many Soldiers turn to religion to strengthen their faith, give their lives greater meaning, and connect with others. At least, that was the gist of what the Catholic priest was saying at the beginning of his homily. Sitting in the pews of the small chapel on Camp Stanley near Uijeongbu in South Korea, I was among about

23 others, including military and a group of nuns from a local convent. We formed the nucleus of Our Lady of Loreto[2]:

> The title Our Lady of Loreto refers to the Holy House of Loreto, the house in which Mary was born, and where the Annunciation occurred, and to an ancient statue of Our Lady which is found there. Tradition says that a band of angels scooped up the little house from the Holy Land, and transported it first to Tersato, Dalmatia in 1291, then Recanati, Italy in 1294, and finally to Loreto, Italy where it has been for centuries. It was this flight that led to her patronage of people involved in aviation.

As declared by Pope Benedict XV on March 24, 1920, and as listed by the Catholic website, "Our Lady of Loreto is the patron saint of pilots, airmen and flight attendants."[3]

Camp Stanley was home to the Aviation Brigade, so naming the post chapel Our Lady of Loreto made sense. The priest asked us to surround ourselves with people of high values like Jesus, Mary, and Loreto, or people who emulated the values and ideals our faith prized. I remember his words: "Your reputation is directly related to the people around you. If you surround yourself with the wrong people, then others associate you and your behavior with them, and, consequently, they influence your actions in a negative way. Build your character base by hanging out with people who share your values." It was during the homily that I decided to strive to surround myself with people of value.

LESSON #28　Leaders put their Soldiers first.

"The junior ranks will board the aircraft first and find a seat of their choice."

I spent my first two weeks in Germany in processing and getting ready to deploy to Bosnia. My aviation unit, 2 Squadron, 6 U.S. Calvary (2-6 Cav, for short) was one of two AH-64 Apache squadrons formed as the 11th Aviation Regiment (Attack). The regiment was V Corps' aerial punching force. The unit and part of each squadron was deployed to Bosnia as part of Operation Joint Forge/Joint Shield. When I arrived to Camp Comanche, I reported to the regiment executive officer (RXO) as ordered. He shook my hand and welcomed me, "Do you want to be the regimental deputy operations officer or the regimental logistics officer?" I had experience in operations at the company and battalion levels at Fort Bragg and at the brigade level in South Korea, so I immediately said I preferred deputy ops. The RXO, a seasoned Major, replied, "That's what I thought. Congratulations! You're the regiment logistics officer."

I later found out his decision was to broaden me as an officer. With three months remaining in the deployment, I had the opportunity to finish planning the redeployment of people and equipment back to Germany as well as lead the overall execution. Since the plans were already approved, I focused on putting the plan into action.

The return to Illesheim, Germany went well with everything and everyone returning safely. Like all Army units, at the conclusion of our redeployment, we conducted an after action review (AAR), which determines how to improve performance by asking, "What was supposed to happen," "What actually happened," and "How can we do better next time?" One of the common themes across the units was Soldiers could have been treated better. The units returned home in phases on U.S. Air Force transport planes with the early phases being heavy with officers. I was so busy planning and executing that I did not notice the imbalance of rank on aircraft. To the credit of the enlisted Soldiers, it was the mid-grade officers, mostly captains, first lieutenants, and chief warrant officer threes who made the comment. I vowed not to let that happen again during my career.

A few months later during the redeployment from Albania to Germany, the Army gave me the opportunity to keep that promise. While our aircraft and most pilots redeployed via air, the remaining personnel and ground equipment moved from Tirana, Albania to Illesheim in four phases. Phase one was a ground convoy from Tirana's airport to the port. Phase two was sea movement on a ship over to Brindisi, Italy. Phase three was rail load operations to move the ground equipment via train back to Illesheim. Phase four was air movement of all remaining personnel via contracted airplane to Frankfurt, followed by bus rentals for the final, three-hour stretch home. I had complete control over planning and execution.

The ship we used was an old transport ferry with rooms varying in sizes. When all the equipment was loaded and secured, I issued the biggest rooms to the most junior of the ranks who helped with loading the equipment. The remaining rooms were assigned by rank with the junior ranks receiving better or bigger rooms. Most of the personnel had no idea there were different room sizes, so there were no complaints.

The regimental leadership knew my plan and fully supported the decision. However, the air movement was not as transparent, as the plane was a contracted 747 with first-class seats. Personnel not involved in the equipment off load from the boat or the load for rail movement waited in a holding area inside a building. When the equipment was safely loaded on the rail cars, I called everyone together. I instructed, "The junior ranks will board the aircraft first and find seats of their choice."

In order, the following ranks boarded to choose their seats: middle enlisted ranks, senior enlisted, junior officer, middle officer, and then senior officer. Quickly, it became apparent the best seats were going to enlisted Soldiers. My decision to put our Soldiers first was questioned by only one individual. The RXO and I quickly shut down the loud, verbal dissent. Along with the RXO and the regimental command sergeant major, I boarded last and took the middle seats for the two-hour flight to Frankfurt. It was the only time I felt good sitting in a middle seat.

LESSON #29 Team success is more important than individual statistics.

10 of 10 Hits

As the commander of 2-6 Cav, I was charged with leading a unit of thirty people, eight AH-64 Apache helicopters, and associated vehicles and ground equipment. The unit personnel included two lieutenants (platoon leaders and pilots), 14 warrant officers (pilots who also served as instructors and oversaw maintenance, safety, and tactics), and 14 enlisted (a first sergeant, two platoon sergeants, and 11 crew chiefs). Shortly after taking command, our annual gunnery qualification was moved up. We had little time to prepare.

My goal was to win the Top Gun Troop for the unit with the highest overall scores. In consultation with my senior instructor pilots, I gave the following guidance: "All crews will qualify twice in the simulator with ten of ten hits and a score of 800 of 1000, and lieutenants will observe sim periods with their pilots." From the silence and odd looks being exchanged, I knew we were in for some pushback. I had been in command less than 30 days, and I just increased the standards for gunnery training. The old standard, according to the gunnery manual, was one qualification simulation period, which meant eight out of ten hits and 700 out of 1000 points. Previously, lieutenants were not required to attend any other simulation periods other than their own practice and qualifying periods. But now, they would observe every pilot in their platoon during the training periods for aerial gunnery. I had drawn a line of what I expected in preparation for our aerial gunnery.

To fire the ammunition and qualify, every pilot, including me, had to meet or exceed the new standard. We had about 45 days until aerial gunnery commenced. Our schedule was grueling. We had to increase our efficiency of using every available simulation period including early mornings, late nights, and Saturdays. The instructor pilots had to change the training scenarios to try to get as much in each two-hour simulation period by focusing only on gunnery skills and nothing else. The instructor pilots, platoon leaders, and I all felt confident we were ready to excel at the squadron's aerial gunnery.

Someone asked me who I thought would win the coveted Top Gun trophy for the highest score by an aircrew. I replied I didn't care about the crew trophy. Army aviation doesn't fight as one aircraft or one crew; we fight in teams like the rest of the Army. We raised our standards to ensure all crews were confident in themselves and their teammates. Thus, we had the highest scores on the range and were the only unit with every crew qualifying on the first run. When we trained for aerial gunnery the following year, the pilots maintained the newly imposed troop standard for aerial gunnery training.

Bravo Troop won the Top Gun Troop for two consecutive years, a feat that had never been accomplished before in the regiment. As a troop commander, unit success is more important than individual success. The Army is an outdoor sports team; great organizations win as a team!

LESSON #30   The power of "What if?"
and "Then What?"

Sleeping in the Big, Red Rental Van

Living in Germany was an incredible blessing, and I counted
the four-year assignment as one of the best locations of my
career. I lived in the state of Bavaria in southern Germany
with a high concentration of Catholics and a feeling of independent conservatism. Often called the Free State of Bavaria,
the region has a significant history of maintaining a level of
independence not provided to most other German states.
From my Army post of Storck Barracks in Illesheim, in a
matter of hours, I could be in a number of other countries
including the Czech Republic, Austria, France, Italy, and
Switzerland.

My older brother and his family expressed an interest
in visiting and experiencing the joys of Europe. So, in the
summer of 1999, I welcomed the five Hincks from Mount
Pleasant, Michigan to Germany. We had a packed schedule
over 14 days with planned trips to areas in Germany, the
Czech Republic, France, and Italy. I rented a big, red van, so
we could travel together. In Italy, we walked Saint Mark's
Square, rode in gondolas down the canals of Venice, visited
the balcony from Romeo and Juliet, experienced a preserved
colosseum in Verona, and toured Vicenza. Our limited time
in France focused on the historic city of Metz, the WWI
battlefield at Verdun, and a quick tour of Strasbourg, an innovative city and the official home of the European Parliament.

The highlights of the Czech Republic were Prague with the old town square, the Charles Bridge, and the beautiful Prague Castle. We even ventured to the Franz Kafka museum. In Germany, we visited the beer gardens in Munich, a concentration camp, the Nazi rally grounds at the Nuremberg Stadium, the walled city of Rothenburg, the castles of Colmburg, Heidelberg castle, and Neuschwanstein. We went on a Rhine river cruise and even had fun at Europa Park.

We developed a solid plan and saw countless sights, but our family vacation was derailed briefly when traffic delays caused us to arrive to our hotel in Ettenheim past midnight. We were surprised to find the hotel doors locked and no lights on. The hotel closed at midnight, as did most hotels in Germany. There were no other hotels open, so the six of us slept in the big, red rental van. We had not done our homework regarding hotel closing times. We suffered for a night with little sleep, the consequences of not planning ahead.

Now, the Army trained me on planning for contingencies if the battlefield doesn't go according to plan. Yet, I failed to apply the key questions of "What if?" and "Then what?" to our family vacation. We still enjoyed a great trip despite sleeping in the big, red rental van for one night.

LESSON #31 How we welcome and say
goodbye speaks volumes.

The Silent Horse Ride in Dress
Uniform with Stetson and Spurs

A hallmark of the best military units is the professional, positive treatment of newly arriving personnel as well as how
people are treated during their departures. Standard operating
procedures describe the welcome and integration plans of
newly arriving personnel and detail the right way to say
goodbye to departing personnel. All new personnel are
hailed, normally at a planned informal dinner where they are
introduced by a sponsor or new boss, and then given the
chance to share a little about themselves and their families.
A farewell is the opposite of a hail. Unit members are praised
for their service with informal gifts like a plaque. Often times,
spouses and families are also recognized for their contribu-
tions. Army units incorporate humor in the hails and farewells
to keep the events light. For prominent members of the organization, farewells can include skits, videos, or special cere-
monies to symbolize the history or lineage of a unit. For
example, the air cavalry on Illesheim wore Stetsons on their
heads, spurs on boots, and flew Apaches, the prominent
attack horse in the fleet of aircraft. Commanders of organizations have a special connection to their people. The self-
sacrifice and family sacrifices every commander makes does
not go unnoticed by the troops.

It was a cool evening on Storck Barracks in Illesheim

when I witnessed a special tribute and farewell to the squadron commander of 6th Squadron, 6th Calvary (6-6 Cav). The tribute began with a knock on the door of the squadron commander's home. He was instructed to put on his dress uniform, Stetson, and spurs. When he next opened his front door, there awaited a horse which he would ride down the road to the officer's club on the opposite end of post. The horse was led by his executive officer, the number two in command, who was silent the entire time.

When the commander approached the final stretch of road to the officer's club, he saw his officers and pilots lined in two rows on opposite sides of the street facing each other. As the commander and horse passed each group of pilots, the two individuals turned to face their commander, silently saluted, then fell in line to walk behind their boss.

How we welcome and say goodbye says much about us. The commander remembers it as a career highlight, and it was the most moving farewell I witnessed.

LESSON #32 When evaluating others, critique the performance, not the person.

The Rules of Being an Observer/Controller

My final assignment in Germany was as an observer/controller (O/C) at the Army's Combat Maneuver Training Center (now called the Joint Maneuver Readiness Center) at Hohenfels. As a senior aviation captain, I was given a highly sought-after job of being an attack O/C, a flying position on the falcon team, which provided mentorship to aviation companies and battalions during training scenarios. I would get to fly and, ultimately, become a pilot-in-command (PC, for short) in the aircraft in which I learned to fly during my rotary wing training at Fort Rucker, Alabama. All O/Cs were instructed in rules governing our behavior during training rotations. The rules for aviation O/Cs included several axioms, but it was the first that made the greatest impact on me: "When evaluating others, critique the performance, not the person."

I saw 16 leaders performing their missions under tough, realistic, and demanding conditions. After a while, it was easy to get jaded. I remember one particular situation when I was observing a captain leading his pilots and Soldiers through a planning exercise. Having already seen eleven similar situations, it seemed as if the captain was repeating some of the same errors as I had seen before. While it was the young officer's first time, I compared him to the other eleven leaders who had gone before him. I was critiquing him against the others, which clearly was not fair. The rule about critiquing the performance and not the person hit me hard in the face and woke me up to the realization that my observations were being influenced by conditions outside of that officer's control. I had to force myself to focus on his performance in relation to the specific situation and not unjustly compare him to others.

As my boss explained to me, the O/C's job was to provide tangible evidence to improve performance based on our observations. The aim was to affect their decision making regardless of the situation or conditions.

LESSON #33 How to think is more important than what to think.

The U.S. Army Command and General Staff College

Fort Leavenworth, Kansas is known for two things: the Army prison and the location of the Army's storied Command and General Staff College (CGSC). Fortunately, I was at Fort Leavenworth for the second reason. I was selected to attend the resident course and would follow in the footsteps of prominent Army officers. The stated mission of CGSC is "educate and train leaders to conduct full spectrum operations in a Joint, interagency, intergovernmental, and multinational environment, and advances the art and science of the profession of arms in order to support the operational requirements of the Army." The CGSC catalog identifies four statements comprising their vision:

1. Intellectual center of excellence.
2. Renowned for study of leadership, conduct of land warfare, and the synchronization and application of all elements of power.
3. Supporting field commanders with well-trained and well-educated leaders, research in the professional body of knowledge, and reach-back planning.

4. World-class faculty dedicated to learning and the advancement of professional knowledge.[4]

Based on elements of reasoning and universal standards in the book *Critical Thinking* by Richard Paul and Linda Elder,[5] all officers at CGSC are trained in critical reasoning and creative thinking. The curriculum provides a wealth of knowledge at a graduate-level of education in groups of 16, which include officers from sister services (Navy, Air Force, Marines, and Coast Guard) and officers from foreign countries. Throughout the ten-month, intensive study program, officers share ideas and develop intellectual skills to practice the profession of arms. How to think through problems is emphasized over what to think. Often times, there are different answers to the same problem, which can be challenging and frustrating. What every student learns is how to think through a problem based on critical reasoning and creative thinking.

An example of how to think through a problem was demonstrated when I was provided a map depicting the area in the Army's National Training Center on Fort Irwin, California and asked how to best defend a specific piece of terrain. The problem caused me to think about what type of enemy I might face, which assets I would need to defend against such an enemy, and how the environment would shape my plan. The thinking process was both linear and non-linear in order to figure out the different conditions and elements affecting my decisions.

The process of how to think through a problem is imperative in conducting combat operations where variables are sometimes not known. It is the emphasis on how to think that produces officers who are competent, innovative, and agile in their solutions.

LESSON #34   Leaders must have confidence in your own work.

"Congratulations, you finally have confidence in your own work."

While attending CGSC, I completed a Master of Military Art and Science (MMAS) degree. The ten-month program was intense with specific milestones including a prospectus finalized by progressively writing and rewriting successive chapters of a thesis. By the ninth month, a full draft thesis was to be completed to leave time for oral competencies and a thesis defense.

My thesis, "Military Leadership and Effective Rhetorical Skills," was the first of its kind at CGSC. I incorporated primary and secondary research to provide a greater understanding of the genre of military rhetoric; I offered methods for leaders to develop effective speech and communication strategies. The Adapted Human Performance Technology (HPT) Model[6] for achieving desired rhetorical skills provided an understanding of the gap between the actual and desired rhetorical skills, the causes of the gap, and solutions to reduce the gap. The Military Rhetorical Skills Model was devised and used as a way to create and measure great speeches. The new model was applied to show how and why speeches are great, specifically how General MacArthur effectively used and created rhetorical eloquence in his farewell address, "Duty, Honor, Country" at West Point in 1962. It showed why Lieutenant Colonel Tim Collins of the Irish Guards 1st Battalion gave a stirring pre-battle speech in March 2003.

I had a superb thesis committee who guided and pushed me, especially my thesis advisor. During the early part of ninth month, almost daily, I met with him to discuss my progress and his edits on my previously submitted work. The cycle of "discuss, rewrite, hand-in, and edit" consumed time, energy, and patience. For the eighth time, we met in his office to discuss my work. Sitting in front of his desk, he slid me a marked-up version of my thesis with his recent edits. I had been writing and rewriting for nine months, but the last month was especially stressful, as I talked with him often because of his recommended changes.

I looked at his edits, put the thesis down, and slid it back to him saying, "I have done what you've asked over the past few weeks, but it seems like you are changing happy to glad and glad to happy. I am done rewriting. My thesis is complete. It is great work. This is what I am handing in for the final time." My thesis advisor smiled, nodded his head, and replied, "Congratulations, you finally have confidence in your own work. Your thesis was ready to be turned a few edits ago, but you weren't ready. It seems like you are now."

Leaders must have confidence in their own work.

LESSON #35   Families are forever.

"Your twin is going to have open heart surgery."

After graduating from CGSC, I was assigned to the 229th Attack Helicopter Regiment, which was my first unit of assignment as new second lieutenant after flight school. The unit was in its seventh month of a twelve-month combat deployment in Afghanistan. I was told I would be assigned as the deputy regiment operations officer. I first reported to Fort Bragg to receive briefings, equipment, and other requirements necessary for combat. After three weeks of preparations, I boarded a commercial flight to Germany to await a military flight into Kuwait for more briefings and equipment before the final flight into Afghanistan. Upon arriving to Kandahar Airfield in southern Afghanistan, I was instructed to call the brigade commander located in the brigade headquarters at Bagram Air Base.

He told me there was a change of plans, and he needed me to be the executive officer (XO) of Task Force Sabre, a battalion-sized aviation unit with a mix of 22 helicopters located in Kandahar. I was in heaven. A choice duty after CGSC for any major is to serve as either an XO or an S3 (operations officer). My primary duties were to oversee the task force's administrative and logistical requirements for combat operations and to plan the operational redeployment from Afghanistan to Fort Bragg. For the next three months, I focused intently on being the best XO in the brigade. I earned my combat spurs since the nucleus of Task Force Sabre was the 1-17 Air Cavalry.

My dream ended abruptly when I received a call from the Red Cross. My twin brother was hospitalized with a potentially life-threatening condition. Immediately, I called back to the States and was told, "John, your twin is going to have open heart surgery." He was involved in a car accident, and in the ER, they discovered a heart defect which, left untreated, could kill him.

I was in a prominent job in one of the best Army aviation units in the world, conducting combat operations. I was conflicted about my decision to leave my unit and Soldiers and return home early. I joined the unit late in their deployment, was just coming up on three months in Afghanistan, and would leave the unit during the critical time of redeployment. Like every leader, I wanted to see my mission through to the end.

Immediately, I told my squadron and brigade commanders. In asking my brigade commander for his approval to leave Afghanistan and return home, he backed me 100 percent, and said, "John, families are forever, so you have to get your ass back home and invest in them during this critical time. Your mission is at home. The unit will survive, but your brother needs you now."

I was home four days later in time to be at my twin's side before and after his surgery. He recovered, and, after short time with him, I returned to Fort Bragg to welcome the unit home.

Despite the demands of combat operations, my chain of

command showed me they truly believe "families are forever."

LESSON #36 Solve the right problem, or create others.

Don't Kill the Dog!

Because I had a Master's of Military Art and Science degree, tactical experience at the battalion and brigade levels, and combat experience from Afghanistan, I was assigned as a tactics instructor at CGSC. I joined the tactics department, but I worked in a teaching team with four other officers and civilians committed to intermediate education of military officers. As part of my certification training, I completed all three phases of the CGSC faculty development program.

In the ten-month period, students attended classes which lasted five hours daily. I taught eighteen classes in those ten months including topics like doctrine fundamentals, full spectrum operations, and a host of other courses. Additionally, I got to serve as tactics instructor for a CGSC-sponsored security assistance visit to the Uzbekistan Military Academy. But my favorite part of teaching was introduction to creative thinking and problem solving.

The lesson plan used David Kolb's experiential learning model. To help anchor the learning, I used the following activity:

Using a six-minute video from the comedic show, *Reno 911!*, I ask students to watch only the first half. It depicts two Reno sheriff deputies approaching a man on the front lawn of a home. The man appears emotionally distraught. The camera pans behind the man to a Basset Hound lying on the ground, head down. When asked what is going on, the man quietly sobs, saying the dog has cancer. The man says he has no money and doesn't know what to do. One of the deputies hugs the man and says it will be alright. Here, I pause the video and ask students to work silently to answer three questions on a sheet of paper: (1) What is the problem? (2) What are the possible solutions to the problem? (3) What is your recommended solution? When they finish, I put them into pairs to discuss their answers. I then have them work in a larger group to find agreement on the answers. I then lead a quick class discussion to record their responses.

Invariably, someone suggests shooting the dog, which causes uneasy laughter. Here, I resume the video. In it, one of the deputies offers to help, quips he once had a dog, and that he knows what to do. The man, overly thankful, remains silent as the deputy walks to the dog, lifts his gun, mumbles "Hey buddy," and then shoots his pistol (presumably shooting the dog, which is not shown). Students, either stunned or laughing, are in disbelief.

The silence on the screen is interrupted by an older lady rushing out of her house next door, asking "What in the heck is going on?" Her tone changes when she looks to where the dog was previously seen and exclaims, "What happened? Who shot my dog?"

The deputy looks confused, but the man points at the lady and sternly states, "I told you to keep your dog off my lawn!" Massive laughter erupts in the classroom. The video classically illustrates the need to understand the problems we are faced with before trying to solve them.

When asked what the real problem is and how they would solve it, the students do several things: they look at the problem from varying viewpoints (man, woman, deputies, even the dog), they examine who truly had a problem before and after the wrong solution was implemented, they analyze how assumptions are made using the ideas of validity and necessity, and they look at the elements of critical reasoning and creative thinking. The teaching point is, "Solve the right problem, or create others." It becomes synonymous with the phrase, "Don't kill the dog."

LESSON #37 Language and culture can empower or impede.

"Was macht die liebe!" and The Slapping Incident

Having lived in foreign countries, here are some of my favorite phrases:
- Carpe diem is Latin for "seize the day."
- Genau is German for "exactly."
- Katchi kapshida is Korean for "we go together!"
- La dolce far niente is Italian for "the beauty of doing nothing."

As a part of pre-deployment training for combat operations in Iraq and Afghanistan, all personnel must complete a cultural understanding course. In Germany and South

Korea, the Army offers language and culture classes as well as country briefings. I've eaten dried squid—the Korean version of popcorn in movie theaters—and sea urchin, which I'll never eat again. Afghan food gave me diarrhea. Iraqi coffee was bitter. I've been attacked by camel spiders in Afghanistan. But it was in Germany where I was tricked into using a phrase by a German friend in a club.

My friend told me the phrase "was macht die liebe" was a cool way to tell a woman she is lovely. A few drinks later, I tried the phrase on German woman. I approached her and confidently said, "Was macht die liebe!" She looked at me quizzically and immediately slapped me. My German friend said something to her in German, and they both laughed.

I later found out the phrase, translated literally, means, "What makes your love," which meant I had asked her how her sex life was. I learned a valuable lesson in how language can empower or impede, depending on competence . . . or incompetence, as the case may be.

LESSON #38 Take the role, job, and mission seriously, but learn to laugh at yourself.

Hinckametrics and HMF in South Korea

There is a running joke in the Army that no one goes to South Korea only twice. We either go once or three times. With fighting two wars in Iraq and South Korea, ongoing deployments loomed large on the Army's horizon. Hence, an assignment to South Korea would keep me away from my family for even longer periods of time. The Army let me help my twin brother during his surgery recovery, but it was time to return to the operational force. Having been a major for over three years with no branch qualifying job as either an operations officer or executive officer, I was behind my peers and my career timeline. Therefore, I volunteered for a second South Korea tour.

I was assigned as the operations officer for 1st Battalion, 2nd Aviation Regiment, one of five battalions in the 2nd Aviation Brigade for the 2nd Infantry Division. Previously, I served as the aviation brigade plans officer, so I had knowledge of aviation operations on the peninsula. As a so-called "double type-A personality," I was intense and mission-focused in executing the training and operations section of the battalion. My take-charge style earned me a reputation in the unit as "the most tactically and technically knowledgeable major in the brigade."

My intensity carried over to the gym. When the unit formed a sports team, we put nicknames on our shirts. The junior officers selected "HMF" for mine. The initials did not mean what most people thought. The term derived from a DJ with the same initials (Hustlin' MuthaF***a), but, for me, it meant "Hinck Master Flex," a reference to my orchestration of battalion operations the way a DJ orchestrates the beats of a song. When I asked a junior officer about the name, he elaborated saying my gym workout routine was jokingly called "Hinckametrics." One promising captain (who now commands an aviation battalion) looked at me and said, "We are just practicing what you always tell us: 'Take your role, job, and mission seriously, but learn to laugh at yourself.'" Indeed, I was the product of my own advice.

CHAPTER 5

Senior-Level Leadership: The Art and Science of Command

LESSON #39 Being smart is the best weapon.

"But we can't fix stupid."

All officers and senior enlisted selected for a battalion-level command positions attend the Army's pre-command course taught at Fort Leavenworth. The three-week course covers topics like leader vision, legal review, and command philosophy; it also features presentations from senior Army leaders with a question-and-answer period. The structure benefits incoming leaders, giving them the necessary time to learn and discuss commanding a tactical formation with strategic implications.

During one of the presentations, a senior officer talked about living in an incredible time where medical advancements and technological innovations make a difference. I took notes in a green notebook and scribbled the following, "If we don't like our physical attributes, we can get a facelift and tummy tuck. We can repair broken limbs and even provide a prosthetic to help the injured walk again. We can repair facial burns suffered in battle. We can do many miracles. But we can't fix stupid." As I developed my command philosophy, I reflected on that thought.

The lesson was about being smart. In the world's most technologically advanced Army, being smart is the best weapon. Being smart meant how to think through problems with critical reasoning and creative thinking or how to take initiative and go to any end for mission success. People are at the forefront of our military, and with the best equipped force on the planet, "Being smart is the best weapon."

LESSON #40 Write to capture ideas, think through issues, and make connections.

My Little Green Book

As a cadet, I was taught to have a pen and paper on me at all times. When getting briefed by an NCO or officer, I was expected to write what I was told. When tired, the human mind may hear, but not truly listen or understand. Writing down instructions and orders helped ensure the message was received and could be referenced immediately.

The Army supply system produced little green books, which measure five by eight inches. They were perfect for taking notes, they slid well into the inside pocket on battle dress uniform pants, and, even wet, they still functioned. I amassed 26 of the little green books, approximately one for every year of my 22 years of service. Using both sides of the page, I had over 4,000 notes.

Many of the stories and lessons in this book were captured in my little green books. Whether issued by the

Army, a set of notecards, a cell phone, or whatever method, the physical act of writing one's thoughts helps capture ideas, think through issues, and make connections.

LESSON #41   Form follows function.

Forming Task Force ODIN-Afghanistan

Being selected to command 3rd Battalion, 214th Aviation Regiment was a highlight of my career. After completing the Army's pre-command and tactical decision making courses at Fort Leavenworth, I reported to Fort Hood in December. I had seven months to train and ready the organization to deploy and join elements already forward in Afghanistan conducting combat operations. The organization, when fully formed, would comprise Task Force ODIN-Afghanistan (TFO-A). My duty description, explained in my officer evaluation report[1], read:

> Commander of 3rd Battalion, 214th Aviation Regiment formed as
> Battalion Task Force ODIN-A, a specialized Aviation Task Force
> providing Reconnaissance, Surveillance, and Target Acquisition
> (RSTA) in direct support to multiple unit commanders from
> Battalion to U.S.AFOR-A for the NATO Coalition's IED-D fight
> in the Afghanistan Theater of Operations. Responsible for the
> readiness and well-being of over 700 soldiers and civilians, and
> their Families, including active, U.S. Army Reserve and U.S. Army
> National Guard components. Responsible for the tactical employ-
> ment of 43 manned and unmanned aircraft that represent the

pinnacle of aviation technology. Integrates emerging technologies and develops tactical employment concepts to support the Commander's mission priorities. Provides command oversight to manage contracts that exceed $600 million annually.

My guiding principle in forming TFO-A was a lesson I learned at CGSC called "form follows function." I saw it up close as the senior aviation O/C and operations officer in the Army's battle command training program. I sought to understand the functions my unit was expected to perform in the pursuit of achieving our assigned missions. Planners in the Army's aviation department at the Pentagon had a good blueprint of what TFO-A was to look like based on a similar organization in Iraq. We worked hard to identify our unit functions and build an organization with the right structure and strategies. My leaders spoke with people who initially built the task force on paper, studied how the TFO in Iraq operated, and went forward to Afghanistan on a pre-deployment site survey to see the conditions and operations the larger task force would play in defeating the IED network.

Over 17 months in command of TFO-A, I worked for three brigade commanders and had two senior raters. My commanders said the following about TFO-A[2]:

> TFO-A is a standards-based, focused, and agile reconnaissance and targeting organization . . . [it] made an immediate impact on finding/defeating enemy networks . . . [it provided] superb multi-air-ground integration and teaming of manned-unmanned assets which resulted in the elimination of over 131 HVIs and 42 IEDs/caches from the battlefield . . . [it] helped ground forces attack and defeat the IED/insurgent networks and protect the populace by providing actionable intelligence . . . TFO-A surpassed

29,000 fixed wing and UAV combat hours and moved over 1100
VIPs via Fixed Wing VIP Detachments.

The TFO-A Soldiers and pilots performed extraordinarily
throughout the entire deployment. Much attention to detail
went into forming TFO-A. The hard work paid off on the
battlefield.

LESSON #42 People need to see leaders up close;
leaders need to see an organization
for situational understanding.

Battlefield Circulation

The only way to know what is going on in an organization is
to circulate. Corporate America coined the phrase "management by walking (or wandering) around."[3] The idea is the
same in the Army, but it is called battlefield circulation. As a
young officer, a trainer at the Army's Joint Maneuver
Training Center and Mission Command Training Center, and
aide to a four-star general, I saw the importance of getting
away from the command post, walking the terrain, checking
on living conditions, conducting missions with Soldiers, and
being available to talk with people.

Despite TFO-A personnel and equipment located at
multiple sites spread across eastern and southern Afghanistan,
I routinely saw every one of the 13 subordinate organizations.
My battlefield circulation was a systematic, scheduled
activity necessary for me to see and understand my Soldiers

and civilians from a perspective only achieved first-hand.

All leaders must circulate regularly. They must position themselves at the right time and place to best influence or understand the conditions. The right plan allows them to see the entire organization. People want to follow someone they believe in, a leader who faces the same dangers they do. Most importantly, people need to see their leaders up close; and leaders need to see their organizations for situational understanding. These lead to effective decision making.

LESSON #43 Leaders make tough calls and write tough letters.

Mr. and Mrs. Johnson, I Am Sorry for Your Loss...

Every Army leader understands the risks associated with war. Every commander wishes to bring home 100 percent of those who are deployed. My wish did not come true.

Three civilians assigned to TFO-A died on a mission in eastern Afghanistan. They were tragically killed when their aircraft exploded to causes still unknown. All three served in military aviation but wanted to make a difference and worked for an aviation company that provided pilots and mission operators for TFO-A's specialized missions. All three were great Americans who left behind loved ones. Their names are on a bracelet I wear daily.

Following positive identification of the aircrew and confirmation of the wrecked plane, I made phone calls to each of the families. It was hard to maintain my composure, as I knew all three individuals and flew with two only a week prior. The mother of one of the deceased crewmembers actually comforted me, saying I shouldn't be sorry for the loss because her son lived his dream, did what he loved, and was probably smiling down on us. After the phone calls, I wrote personal letters to each family to express my condolences and my gratitude for their loved ones' service.

The Army instills in every leader to make the tough calls and write the tough letters. Still, I hope I never have to do that again.

LESSON #44 Plan and rehearse transitions as early as possible.

"John, you're leaving command early to be a general's aide."

The TFO-A was the only unit of its kind in the Afghanistan theater of operation, and its 40-plus assets were unique. Hence, the aircraft remained in Afghanistan, but the people were replaced on phased rotation. My redeployment date, along with most of the unit which trained in the States as the unit stood up, was mid-July, 12 months after arriving into Afghanistan.

In March of 2010, my replacement was identified with a planned overlap in late June. The transition plan, called left seat, right seat ride, was where the incoming commander shadowed the outgoing commander and observed the decisions, battle rhythm, and unit operations to gain situational understanding. The second half of the transition occurred when the incoming commander performed crucial duties with the outgoing commander beside to validate the actions and decisions.

In March, with 120 days until redeployment, I instructed TFO-A personnel to plan the right seat, left seat ride. I wanted briefings on the transition plans for all leadership positions. My boss asked for the same from me, which was a great idea. I had my XO stand in for the incoming commander as we walked through my own transition plan. I was comfortable in planning and conducting my plan, but my brigade commander wanted to ensure all leader transitions would be planned and rehearsed at every level.

In April, I was selected to serve as the aide to a four-star general. I was to leave in late May to return stateside, which was two months early from command and combat. Since the incoming commander was not to arrive until June, I handed the battalion reins to my XO, a capable and competent senior major. We were only able to transition smoothly and effectively because we planned and rehearsed as early as possible.

LESSON #45 With a foundation of standards and discipline, goals should be specific, objective, and measurable.

Winning the Fixed Wing Unit of the Year Award

By our second year and after our first 12 months in combat, I wanted 3-214th Aviation Regiment (formed as Task Force ODIN-Afghanistan) to win the Army's Fixed Wing Unit of the Year Award. I had every confidence we would excel on the battlefield because the Army invested in the right equipment and cutting-edge technology to make a major impact against the IED network. My initial concern was not on the battlefield, but during the seven months of train-up conducting decentralized operations at multiple training locations.

Poor decisions and Army standards and discipline violations prevented deployments and caused training delays. As commander, my aim was to build an organization based on standards and competent teamwork to rapidly integrate and help defeat the IED network in Afghanistan. We needed to abide by the Army Strong motto of immense mental, physical, and emotional strength, and we needed to uphold the Army value of honor, which was emblematic of our ability to meet other Army values.

During weekly safety briefings, I had one rule: "Don't die." We could survive all else. Suicides, DUIs, and alcohol-related incidents were rising on Fort Hood. I wanted to communicate to my Soldiers that I cared about them and expected them to train for combat, but I would not tolerate unnecessary risks while off duty. We had to prevent, not just reduce, accidents and incidents.

During the seven months of training and certification at Fort Hood, 3-214th Aviation Regiment had the fewest incidents of any other battalion on post. We deployed to combat with 100 percent of assigned personnel and equipment, which were essential to Afghanistan's operational tempo. The success was attributable to the great NCOs and junior leaders in the organization, and, ultimately, the best disciplined Soldiers on the base. Our goals were specific, objective, and measurable. Due to our integrity, TFO-A won the Army's 2010 Fixed Wing Unit of the Year Award.

LESSON #46 There is only one chance to make a first impression.

"What keeps you up at night?"

Before taking command of the Minneapolis recruiting battalion, I attended a three-week recruiting pre-command course hosted by the U.S. Army recruiting command. The 20 incoming battalion commanders and battalion command sergeant majors were trained in the doctrine and principles of leading a recruiting organization to meet the Army's manning requirements. We had the opportunity to listen to speakers who were either in recruiting leadership positions or from the chain of command to provide their insights and guidance about recruiting operations.

One Army senior leader asked what was on our minds. No hands were raised. No questions were asked. The awkward silence continued until my hand went up. Heads turned. After the nonverbal cue to proceed, I asked, "What keeps you up at night?" This question wasn't my idea. I heard it from a fellow officer who asked the question three years prior while I was at Fort Leavenworth.

The General kept my gaze, pondered the question, and answered, "Last night, what kept me up was wondering if anyone would ask a good question." Smiling, he continued, "Thank you for being bold and meaningful with your simple question." He proceeded to share both personal and professional concerns. He spoke about family, Soldiers, garrison, combat, suicides, health, and fitness. For nearly 30 minutes, the audience got an honest and straightforward account of what keeps an Army senior leader up at night.

At the end of his remarks, he looked in my direction and concluded, "You only get one time to make a first impression. The questions you ask are a reflection of your intellect, so ask smart ones."

LESSON #47 To make decisions, we must see situations with our own eyes.

The First 90 Days in Command

The following story shows my actions within the first three

months of being placed in the senior leadership role of an Army organization. The position is similar to a chief executive officer. What follows were my findings after my first 90 days in command of the Minneapolis Recruiting Battalion:

My initial impressions were formed prior to taking command including two visits to the unit at key events based on my predecessor's guidance, PCC (Pre-Command Course) attendance, and the official right seat, left seat ride. With full access to the unit's products and several discussions and study of recruiting doctrine, my initial impression was the Eagle Battalion exemplified a disciplined formation, dedicated to warrior ethos and Army values with competent staff. The organization was successful in many areas, but not all personnel could articulate the reasons for success. Hence, I strove to understand if the success was by luck or design, the latter being the imperative to replicate continued success. The unit had room for improvement in HQ functionality, management of resources, command decisions based on priorities, MAP (Mission Accomplishment Plan) discipline/compliance, future soldier (FS) program management, physical fitness, training management, event planning, and synergistic use of all available assets focused on priority efforts based on Army and community needs. The causes of the challenges centered on not doing the right things, not doing the right things right, or not doing enough of the right things right. While I did not want to rush to change, I believed I needed to act immediately to modify behavior in four areas:

1) Strengthen the esprit de corps across the ranks of

military and civilians based on our Army values of treating all with dignity and respect and being balanced professionals.

2) Build a healthy funnel (pool) for meeting our assigned recruiting mission founded on the key functions of the station and team recruiting.

3) Execute meaningful, purposeful events built upon a focused-fusion concept in meeting the collective needs of the Army, community, and schools.

4) Change how we approach communities and schools from being seen as "taking kids away" to "being a giving guest" and fostering partnerships while emphasizing that "families are forever."

These areas were the foundation of my initial command guidance and further developed based upon input from the battalion's command sergeant major, the senior enlisted NCO in the unit.

After taking command, I briefed all commanders, 1SGs, station commanders, and all staff on this vision. Additionally, I visited all 43 stations and nearly 300 Soldiers and civilians across the 290,000 square miles comprising Minnesota, Iowa, North Dakota, South Dakota, Wisconsin, and Illinois. I spent the first eight days in the HQ to form the staff and provide guidance to meet my expectations during my travels. The next 90 days I spent on the road visiting the entire footprint. Based on my observations, the unit needed to focus on three areas for mission improvement:

1) Volume production and regaining market share, specifically in regular Army senior alphas and in Army Reserve graduate alphas and prior service categories.
2) Future Soldier retention, FS loss inside of 30 days, and FS referrals. We needed to conduct better, thorough hot seats and improve our applicant packets before going to MEPS (Military Entrance Processing Station).
3) Building a healthy funnel with the best qualified applicants. While we identified the root causes as declined enlistment and medical, we needed to recruit more qualified applicants through precision targeting and take losses closer to the 33-day mark.

I knew my unit and what needed improvement. I confidently and competently discussed my observations and command decisions. To make those decisions, I needed to see it all for myself.

LESSON #48 Changing identity and culture starts with values.

Strength and Honor! Eagle Strong!

Military personnel traditionally greet each other by exchanging salutes and words. The words are symbolic of the unit motto or mission. The title "Strength and Honor" was how we greeted each other in both the aviation and recruiting battalions I commanded. "Strength" meant to live up the Army Strong motto of "showing immense physical, mental, and moral strength to make a difference that matters." And "Honor" meant living up to all Army values. The return words "Eagle Strong" signified the other individual would do the same thing and, together, the Eagle Battalion would be strong.

For the first six months, I visited every one of the 54 recruiting locations in four states, discussed my command philosophy, and explained the words, "Strength and Honor! Eagle Strong!" Soldiers understood the guidance. Those who weren't in the unit laughed.

When I took over, the battalion was ranked eighth of eight in the brigade and 34th of 38 battalions nationwide. Six months later, we ranked first in the brigade and sixth in the nation. People weren't laughing anymore.

We simply changed how we talked to each other, which influenced behavior and put us on track to do the right things right. We had the least number of poor behaviors in the brigade. That meant we could shift to changing how we conducted recruiting operations, built community partnerships, and informed the teachers and parents about Army opportunities, all to put people in uniform which was the real mission of the recruiting battalion. Cultural change required simple and meaningful methods to anchor the new words into the organization's spirit. Changing culture is like eating an elephant; it takes one bite at a time. Changing organizational identity and culture starts with values. When values are the bedrock of the organization, behavior improves, and the unit can move toward other improvements.

A few years ago, Lambda Chi Alpha, an international Greek-letter fraternity, fundamentally changed the culture of their organization by implementing a values-based program. They saw a rise in membership, reduction in poor behaviors, and led other fraternities in standards and disciplines. "Developed in 2007 and modeled after the U.S. Army's values, Lambda Chi Alpha's Seven Core Values — loyalty, duty, respect, service and stewardship, honor, integrity, and personal courage — provide a moral compass for members of the Fraternity."[4] Clearly, Lambda Chi Alpha leads with values. Those values form the basis for building leadership and strengthening character.

LESSON #49 To achieve success, we must improve the value of our people or remove them from the team.

"...they are occupying a seat, weighing you down, and not singing your fight song."

I once heard a fellow battalion commander advise, "You have to get the wrong people off your bus because they are occupying a seat, weighing you down, and not singing your fight song." When I took command of the Minneapolis recruiting battalion, there were 21 personnel who violated legal, moral, or recruiting standards, leaving approximately 85 percent of assigned personnel responsible for 100 percent of the work. With that ratio, we would never achieve our mission.

Due to Army-wide reduction in resources and personnel, my unit faced cuts and constraints on work hours. I needed every position filled with capable people who could contribute to achieving the mission. So, we fought hard to get the wrong people off the bus and free up a seat for the right people to board. The unit had mostly superstars, people with positive value who rolled us forward. Those with negative value were slowing momentum.

A handful of people were, essentially, resting their hands on the stop cord, teetering on the verge of stopping our unit's momentum. They weren't performing to standard, but they weren't causing issues. We had to pull them back, improve their worth, or risk losing them at their next stop, likely a bad decision. Fundamentally, we had to change the culture with haste.

LESSON #50   People join organizations for many reasons, but they stay for three: they feel able to make a difference, they feel trusted, and they feel valued.

Future Soldier Retention

My battalion had a problem retaining Future Soldiers in the formation. When I took over, we had a 22 percent loss rate with a standard of 10 percent. The reasons for dropping from the ranks were legal problems, apathy, or medical issues. We fixated on preventing losses by focusing on negative aspects. I decided to change how we talked about FS Retention by finding out what made the FS stay in the formation. My goal was to retain 90 percent or higher.

When people aim to join the Army, they pass the required tests and medical screenings and become a future soldier for four to seven months before basic training. Each FS prepares for basic training by completing physical fitness assessments, a basic training task list, a referral program, and projected job research. Part of the problem was we didn't know why people were staying. So, step one was to find out and correlate that information with positive FS retention.

My staff discovered three common reasons: FS felt they were part of something bigger that made a difference, they felt trusted, and they felt valued. So, we modified our FS program to emphasize 1) making sure they felt like a part of a team with positive community impact through team completion of the basic training task list and physical training, 2) making individuals feel trusted within the organization by developing their referral skills and assigning FS leadership positions, and 3) making every effort to show we valued them through promotions, Facebook announcements, and hometown news releases.[5]

The positive focus on making FS feel included, trusted, and valued paid off. Eight months later, our FS retention rates were 92 percent.

LESSON #51   Building partnerships to make
a difference requires common
ground and common reasons.

Only One Out of Every Four American Youth are Qualified to Join the Military

Lack of physical fitness, sedentary lifestyles, poor eating habits, and childhood obesity are threatening our national security. Less than 25 percent of American youth are qualified to join the military.[6] Most people want to make a positive impact on our nations' youth and communities.

Using this approach, the Minneapolis recruiting battalion joined efforts with Century Community College, Des Moines Area Community College, SkillsUSA, the YMCA, and numerous high schools to create health and fitness expos. At the expos, local community organizations came together in high school gyms to talk with and show youth and teachers about mental, physical, and emotional fitness. Together, these organizations built social capital in communities.

The Army led in building meaningful, purposeful events using a focused-fusion concept in meeting the collective needs of the Army, community, and schools. We changed how we approached those community and schools, and their attitudes changed toward us. We were now seen as Soldiers who cared about students and their health. Two years later, the likelihood that youth would join the military, increased in the upper Midwest, the first time an increase occurred in quite some time.

Building partnerships requires finding the common ground and giving people a common reason to make a difference.

LESSON #52   NCOs (Non-Commissioned Officers) are the backbone of our military.

The NCO Motto: "Be, Know, Do"

It has been said the strength of our nation is our Army, the strength of our Army is our Soldiers, and the strength of our Soldiers is our families. The NCOs of the U.S. military are the best in the world. They exemplify their motto of "Be, Know, Do." Simply, "Be" includes their values and attributes, "Know" equates to their skills, and "Do" exemplifies their actions.[7] The U.S. military gives more authority to NCOs than any other military because they are the best trained and the best at accomplishing the task to standard regardless of conditions. They live by the NCO Creed[8]:

> No one is more professional than I. I am a noncommissioned officer, a leader of Soldiers. As a noncommissioned officer, I realize that I am a member of a time honored corps, which is known as "The Backbone of the Army." I am proud of the Corps of noncommissioned officers and will at all times conduct myself so as to bring credit upon the Corps, the military service and my country regardless of the situation in which I find myself. I will not use my grade or position to attain pleasure, profit, or personal safety.
>
> Competence is my watchword. My two basic responsibilities will always be uppermost in my mind—accomplishment of my mission and the welfare of my Soldiers. I will strive to remain technically

and tactically proficient. I am aware of my role as a noncommissioned officer. I will fulfill my responsibilities inherent in that role. All Soldiers are entitled to outstanding leadership; I will provide that leadership. I know my Soldiers and I will always place their needs above my own. I will communicate consistently with my Soldiers and never leave them uninformed. I will be fair and impartial when recommending both rewards and punishment.

Officers of my unit will have maximum time to accomplish their duties; they will not have to accomplish mine. I will earn their respect and confidence as well as that of my Soldiers. I will be loyal to those with whom I serve; seniors, peers, and subordinates alike. I will exercise initiative by taking appropriate action in the absence of orders. I will not compromise my integrity, nor my moral courage. I will not forget, nor will I allow my comrades to forget that we are professionals, noncommissioned officers, leaders!

I know they are the best because they taught me, like every officer, throughout an entire career, and I stood beside them in combat. Nearly every lesson I learned has come from observing an NCO or being mentored by one.

CHAPTER 6

Executive-Level Leadership: Observing Lifelong Learning

LESSON #53 Actions are reflections of supervisor and organization.

"Have the perspective of a duck."

The day I was selected as the aide to a four-star general, I was on Bagram Air Base in the eastern part of Afghanistan having just returned from some R&R. To serve as an aide was an honor, but it would take me out of combat and battalion command early. The decision would impact my battalion, but the Army had other requirements for me. I immediately informed my brigade commander. As a former aide to a general, he gave me this advice: "Have the perspective of a duck."

Seeing my puzzled look, he explained, "You ever see a duck on water? It looks calm and collected, gliding above the water. But what's not seen are its feet moving like crazy below the surface. Whether as an aide or a senior leader, you must always look calm and collected. As a leader, your actions and words are a reflection of your organization. As an aide, you are the alter ego of your boss. So, make sure you always have the perspective of a duck."

LESSON #54 The power of "why."

What Two-Year Olds and General Officers Have in Common?

I served for a year as the four-star general's aide. In that position, I was able to see the Army from an incredible vantage point, to observe senior Army leaders interacting and executing their duties at executive levels. At the same time, my twin brother was raising his son. The kid had a beautiful curiosity about him, asking questions about everything.

What struck me was two-year olds and general officers had one commonality; they both asked "Why?" They asked it a lot.

Kids asked "Why?" because they were curious about life and had not yet been conditioned to accept things as they appeared. Senior leaders asked why because they were conditioned to get to the root cause of a problem and influence the outcome efficiently and effectively. We should ask away and discover the power of "why."

LESSON #55 Want something of value?
Work hard for it.

"There's no free chicken!"

We all have phrases we're known for saying. For me, statements like "Strength and Honor!" and "Make a difference!"

conclude emails or letters. "Strength" (living up to the "Army Strong" motto), "Honor" (representing Army values), and "Make a difference" (do something that matters) embody my personality.

There was a time when saloons attracted customers by advertising "free lunch," as the real money was made in alcohol purchases:

> It was into this context that the economic theorists enter the fray and 'there's no such thing as a free lunch' is coined. It isn't known who coined the phrase. It certainly wasn't the economist Milton Friedman, who was much associated with the term. He was a celebrated Nobel Prize-winning economist and his monetarist theories were highly influential on the Reagan and Thatcher administrations in the 1980s and 90s. Friedman certainly believed that 'there's no such thing as a free lunch' and he published a book with that title in 1975, but wasn't, and never claimed to be, the originator of the phrase.[1]

In a nod to the saying, "There's no such thing as a free lunch," I once overheard a senior leader utter the statement, "There's no free chicken!"

Nothing is free, neither lunch nor chicken. If we want something of value, we must work hard for it.

LESSON #56 Treat others better than they think they should be treated.

Redefining the Golden Rule

A close friend of mine is the CEO and owner of a brand experiences agency called Bishop-McCann. He built his organization and life on a principle that has clarity in purpose and a singular focus on making people feel special.

The Golden Rule—"do unto others as you would have others do unto you"—has long been interpreted as treat people how you want to be treated. My friend's attitude and actions redefine the Golden Rule.

Whether with employees, customers, family, or friends, he treats others better than they think they should be treated. He goes beyond expectations. He exceeds the standard in every regard. Redefining the Golden Rule can help us be better people and build great lives, too.

LESSON #57 Squaring our actions.

Honoring the Life of a Brother

While visiting a cemetery to pay respects to my mother who died of cancer when I was a child, I noticed a funeral a short distance away. Besides someone holding an open bible, who I assumed was a priest or pastor, there was a group of Masons dressed in suits, each wearing a Masonic apron. I watched as they performed a short ceremony to honor the deceased. Following the final blessings, I approached one of the Masons and inquired about the deceased.

"We don't really know him," he said, "but he was a fellow Mason and had served during WWII. As a Mason, we are taught to square our actions. Our Masonic brother passed, and he doesn't have any immediate family. We came here to honor the life of a brother."

A Masonic website states:

> The Square is prominent throughout the rituals and ceremonies of Freemasonry and is one of the first symbols introduced and explained to the Freemason. During the initiation ceremony, the new Freemason is told the Square should remind him to conduct his life upon the square, indicating moral and ethical behavior. During the Lecture, the Square is described as part of the Furniture of the Lodge dedicated to the Master, as it is the Masonic emblem of his office. It is also one of the six Jewels of the Lodge, teaching morality. The Square is also identified as one of the Working Tools of the Fellowcraft Mason, where it admonishes the Freemason to square his "actions by the Square of Virtue."[2]

I have been a Mason for over 25 years but never experienced the true meaning of squaring our actions until that fall morning at my mother's grave.

LESSON #58 Time to think.

Executive Time on the Schedule

Military officers, like most leaders, want to get as much done as possible in a day. As the general's aide, I wanted to maximize my boss's schedule and ensure his time wasn't wasted. When planning schedules, we tend to pack as much as possible into a day. The first time I planned a schedule for my boss it was detailed and coordinated with every minute accounted for on a trip.

In showing the trip itinerary to the executive officer, he advised me to add something called "executive time" on the schedule for preparation before a meeting or at night for personal time. The executive officer added, "Every leader needs time to think, or we go from meeting to meeting with little time to reflect on decisions." In our busy activities of work and life, we need time to think and time to think about how we think.

LESSON #59 Honesty is the best policy; if we stand our ground, it will set us free.

"Are you with me or against me?"

Toxic leadership is at the forefront of leadership studies in military and academia[3]. Fortunately, in 22 years, I experienced little toxicity from my Army leaders. I did, however, experience screaming and harsh words, which are understandable in combat situations.

During one deployment, I had a boss who, when upset over a contentious issue, would demand, "Are you with me or against me?"

At the beginning of, what would be, a long budget meeting, my boss mentioned a controversial budget allocation issue and ended his statement with, "Are you with me or against me?"

I responded, "Sir, it looks like I'm against you on this one. We may have to agree to disagree."

He stared back at me for what seemed like long, empty minutes. Slowly, he said, "John, you're the first person to go against me. I appreciate your honesty. You are excused from this staff meeting." Then, turning to the assembled group in the conference room, he quipped, "Honesty is the best policy. Learn to stand your ground, and the truth will set you free."

I found out later he decided in my favor on the budget issue.

LESSON #60   Don't hand off a fixable problem to the boss.

Why Dad Tied Our Shoes, but the Boss Doesn't

While working as the senior aviation O/C in the U.S. Army Battle Command Training Program, I observed interactions between many officers in units ranging from brigade to three-star level commands. In the exchange between a junior officer and a senior officer, I overheard the following discussion:

"Captain Green, your work is incomplete. Make these corrections, and return to me." The young officer continued returning with a new product only to receive the same advice every time. On the ninth time, the senior officer said, "Who taught you to tie your shoes?"

The younger officer answered, "My father, sir."

"Well, good. I figured it was one of your parents," said the senior officer, who followed with "Do you expect me to tie your shoes?"

Confused, the junior officer replied, "No, sir, why do you ask?"

The senior officer answered, "When you were a kid and you didn't know how to tie your own shoe, your father tied your shoe. Through practice, you learned how to tie your own shoe and then didn't need to go to your father. So, when you bring work that is incomplete, I'm going to make you practice until you can do it on your own. At some point, you will have learned enough through practice to know you don't give your boss a problem you can fix."

LESSON #61 Saying thanks must be genuine, specific, and timely.

Writing Four-Star Letters

As the general's aide, I partook in visits to several locations and units across the Army. Following every visit, I drafted thank you notes based on discussions with my boss or on my observations of the visit. Every note contained something genuine and specific to the leader and unit we visited. Within 24 hours of the visit, the notes, signed by my boss, were in the mail. In one year, my boss visited over 60 units and leaders worldwide. After every visit, thank you notes were sent without fail.

With today's computer-mediated communication, rarely are thank you notes ever sent or received. Implicitly, I learned saying thanks must be genuine, specific, and timely.

LESSON #62 Leaders do more than contribute; they commit to their people.

The Chicken and the Pig

The Army is a people business and outdoor sport. Taking care of soldiers and families and achieving missions are at the heart of what the best leaders do daily. Attitude is critical in approaching the level of commitment all leaders should possess.

While visiting a unit that was training for an upcoming deployment at the National Training Center in Fort Irwin, California, I heard a great explanation about how a leader should think about their level of commitment. A unit commander in a meeting with his subordinate leaders, stated, "I need all of you fully committed to this mission." He turned to a subordinate who struggled to complete his assignment in the previous mission, and said, "I saw you eating bacon and eggs this morning. Do you know the difference between bacon and eggs?"

Dumbfounded, the subordinate answered "No."

The commander wryly said, "The chicken contributed while the pig committed. I need you to be a pig out there. I need you and your team fully committed."

LESSON #63 Practice to find strength and honor.

A Key to the Dojo and
Receiving My Green Belt

Years ago during my first assignment to Fort Bragg, North Carolina, I began practicing Tang Soo Do, a Korean martial art influenced by Chinese and Japanese principles. My older brother practiced the art, and I saw Chuck Norris movies, which popularized the style in the Western world. I attended classes three to four nights a week under the guidance of a black belt master who served in the military. He was an extraordinary teacher and philosopher.

The color rankings were white, yellow, orange, green, purple, red, and black. After a few months, I earned my yellow belt by demonstrating forms, attacking and defending techniques, and oral knowledge. Due to my athletic ability, he often demonstrated moves or takedown techniques using me as the counterpart. After training for about five months, he called, "Mr. Hinck, please come forward." I sighed as I got up and moved to position in front of him. He repeated multiple techniques on me to the point of my exhaustion.

At the conclusion of class, he asked to see me in his office. He told me to sit and addressed me, "Mr. Hinck, do you know why you are sore?" Not waiting for an answer, he continued, "You have the physical strength, but not the mental or emotional strength yet, but in practice, you will get stronger. Mr. Hinck, do you know why I call you forward for demonstrations?" Again, not waiting for me to speak, he offered, "It is because I want the other students to know that it is you I trust enough to help teach techniques and impart the wisdom of the art. It is an honor for you to be with me in front of the class. Your silence is expected. I ask that you respect my decision more in the future." I was humbled. Yet my master had more to say. "John, you are one of my best and most promising students. I offer you a key to the dojo, so you can practice more." I felt a trust beyond explanation. My attitude changed. The key to the dojo allowed me to practice late at night or on weekends to work around my job. I spent much time practicing my forms and techniques alternating between fast execution, slow execution, strong execution, and combining the methods to perfect the form.

In my eighth month of training after much practice, I tested for the next level, an orange belt. With the entire class observing, I demonstrated six forms and self-defense techniques, sparred with two red belts, showed basic fighting techniques using the bow staff, demonstrated ability to break three-quarter inch board, and answered questions about general knowledge, culture, and terminology. The toughest part was sparring with the two red belts, but I managed to not get knocked down. The entire test took 40 minutes.

When the time came for awarding of the belt, my master presented me with a green belt stating this was only the second time he skipped a gup (level) in awarding a belt. As he presented me with the green belt, he leaned forward and said, "Continue to practice to find your own strength and honor." I learned that pursuing knowledge and strength is the honorable way to attain rank. Before I departed Fort Bragg, I learned Nai Ahn Chi Cho Dan and was both Pyingahn Yi Dan and Bassai along with more bow staff techniques.[4] I continue practicing the martial arts and hope to one day enter midnight blue or black belt ranks.

After my 22 years of active duty service in the U.S. Army, I rediscovered the lesson to "practice to find your own strength and honor" when I started CrossFit. Through the on-ramp portion which all new CrossFit students must complete, I learned one can find a level of self-worth through hard work and sweat by building core muscle groups and getting fit for life. I rediscovered my physical and mental strength in a new workout that challenged me in new ways.

Finding our strength and honor occurs at home, in church, in a uniform, in a classroom, in a dojo, or in a gym. Most importantly, strength and honor starts with us. We must continue to find our strength in honorable ways.

LESSON #64 Leadership is about knowing and accepting yourself.

The Running Father

In the New Testament, Luke Chapter 15, the story of the lost or prodigal son has great meaning within the Christian faith. As the son is returning home, the father runs to him, embraces him, and welcomes him back. I focused on the image of this father running to his son. Years later, a friend would describe this verse as the tale of "The Running Father." The story demonstrates how the word "agape" is used to show a father's unconditional love for his son. It illustrates God's fatherly love for humans.

This type of love is the example for loving thy neighbor. The Greeks used the term to denote a pure love for a spouse or family member. I found out later the Order of DeMolay further defined agape as "love for no other reason than for the sake of being." How my father demonstrated agape is blended with the meanings from the Bible, the Greeks, and DeMolay.

When my mother was dying, it was my father who worked all day, stayed with her at night, and spent most weekends attending to her in the hospital. My dad used to say, "Cancer killed your mom, but God saved her." At 13, I needed that idea, as I struggled to understand why God would allow my mother to die. When my twin brother was lost and returned home, it was my father who ran to him, embraced him, and welcomed him back into the family.

My father has always been there for our family. It is through his unconditional love that I was able to quit running from a part of me that was tough to accept. Growing up and through most of my adult life, I have struggled with accepting my true self. I hid my true identity and played the part that others expected. Despite the Army's emphasis on conformity, it was peculiarly in the Army as a commissioned officer and Apache helicopter pilot that I had the opportunity to experience other cultures and viewpoints regarding creativity and sexuality. I started to think about how to share who I really was with others. Yet I had been accustomed to living within the bounds of others' expectations, within the rules of the Catholic Church, and within the military's official "Don't Ask, Don't Tell" policy. The policy had been in existence most of my career. There were no role models of gay military leaders. My last year of service is when I truly started to accept being gay to family and friends.

When I found the courage to tell my father, he said, "Yeah, I know son. I love you. I am happy you could finally trust me." When I asked how he knew, he responded, "Well, I'm your father. I'm not dumb." It was hard to cry and laugh at the same time. When I spoke of dreams and making decisions, my father listened and always said, "You can do it" and "I love you for who you are." The weight of the world seemed to be lifted off of my shoulders. He knew not of my limits or faults, but of my possibilities and my strength as we both accepted who I am. As I shared it with others, I felt a renewed freedom. I didn't have to hide from others, and I could have an honest relationship built on full openness and fidelity.

My father continues to run today. It is his unconditional love that serves as the foundation for who I am. Knowing and accepting oneself is not an easy path sometimes, but all leaders must discover who they really are so they can start running for themselves. Strength and Honor is about finding your true strength and living in that strength in an honorable way.

www.johnmhinck.com

124

NOTES

Chapter 2

1. Retrieved November 18, 2013, from the WWII Database website: http://www.ww2db.com.

2. Hinck, J. (2001, December 18). *The Book of Ed: My Father's POW Story.* Unpublished work.

3. U.S. Senate. (1975, July 8). President Gerald Ford signed H.R. 2946, "A bill for the relief of Mrs. Dorothy Hinck" thus enacting Private Law 94-14.

4. *Building Tomorrow's Leaders Today Since 1919.* Retrieved December 2, 2013, from DeMolay International website: http://www.demolay.org.

5. Headquarters, Department of the Army. (2001, November 1.) Field Manual 3-0, *Operations.*

Chapter 3

1. Russell Ackoff is credited with first proposing the DIKW model showing the link between Data-Information-Knowledge-Wisdom in his 1988 address to the *International Society for General Systems Research* and published in his article "From Data to Wisdom" in the *Journal of Applied System Analysis* (1989).

2. Hinck J. (2014). The "What? So What? Now What?" of wise decision making. *Celebrate Innovation Magazine*, Special Edition-Celebrate Innovation Week 2014, pp. 21-24.

3. The ideas of "to know and train subordinates at least two levels down" and "fully understand the commander's intent two levels up" are found in the following *Army manuals*: ADRP 6-22, *Army Leadership*, August 2012 (pp. 6-1, 8-2, and 10-3),

in FM 6-22, Army Leadership, October 2006 (pp. 7-15 and 11-4), and in ADRP 7-0 *Training Units and Developing Leaders*, August 2013 (pp. 2-5).

4. Headquarters, Department of the Army. (2012, May). ADRP 5-0, *The Operations Process*, pp. 2-9 and 2-19-20.

5. In circumstances where service members commit lesser crimes, they can choose non-judicial punishments administered by a commanding officer or proceed to trial by court martial. The process and protections are discussed under Section 815, Article 15, Commanding Officer's Non-Judicial Punishment in Part 03-Non-Judicial Punishment of the Uniform Code of Military Justice.

Chapter 4

1. *Foal Eagle*. Retrieved January 14, 2014, from Wikipedia: http://en.wikipedia.org/wiki/Foal_Eagle.

2. *Our Lady of Loreto*. Retrieved January 16, 2014, from Saints.SPQN.com – notes about your extended family in heaven website: http://saints.sqpn.com/our-lady-of-loreto.

3. *Our Lady of Loreto Patron Saint*. Retrieved January 16, 2014, from Catholic Online website: http://www.catholic.org/saints/patron.

4. CGSC Vision. Retrieved January 8, 2014, from U.S. Army Command and General (CGSC) website: http://usacac.army.mil/cac2/cgsc.

5. Paul, Richard and Elder, Linda. (2011). Critical Thinking. New Jersey: Prentice Hall.

6. Hinck, J. (2012). *Military Leadership and Effective Rhetorical Skills*. Biblio Scholar.

Chapter 5

1. The excerpts regarding the forming of TF ODIN were taken from duty descriptions as described in three of my Officer Evaluation Reports between dates of December 2008 through May 2010.

2. The excerpts regarding the performance of TF ODIN were taken from comments by superior officers as described in three of my Officer Evaluation Reports between dates of December 2008 through May 2010.

3. The term Management by Walking Around (MBWA) was first coined by Tom Peters and Robert Waterman in their 1982 book, In *Search of Excellence*. Additionally, the term experienced a resurgence in 2012 and 2013 by *Harvard Business Journal* and *Fortune Magazine*.

4. Seven Core Values of Lambda Chi Alpha. Retrieved January 24, 2014, from the Lambda Chi Alpha website: https://www.lambdachi.org/true-brother/seven-core-values.

5. U.S. Army Recruiting Battalion-Minneapolis. (2013, May 6). *Updated Future Soldier Standard Operating Procedures (SOP)*, pp 12-13.

6. The figure of less than 1 in 4 of our nation's youth are qualified to join the U.S. military ranks was derived from a combination of three studies: Woods & Pool 2012 Population Estimates; Lewin Group 2007 Study; developed by U.S. Army Accessions Command G2/9, Center for Accessions Research (502-613-0556). The alarming statistic has been called a national security issue for the United States. The information is also found in recurring talking points from the U.S. Army Recruiting Command.

7. The NCO motto of "Be, Know, Do" is best described in the Department of the Army's Field Manual 22-100, *Army Leadership*.

8. The U.S. Army NCO Creed is found in many publications and study guides, but FM 7-22.7 *The U.S. Army NCO Guide* (2002, December 23) best describes the history, purpose, and meaning of the famous paragraphs.

Chapter 6

1. Retrieved January 3, 2014, from the Phrases.org website: http://www.phrases.org.uk/meanings/tanstaafl.html.
2. *The Tools of Masonry.* Retrieved December 14, 2013, from the Masonic Trowel website: http://www.themasonictrowel.com.
3. Reed, George E. (2004). Toxic leadership. *Military Review*, July-August 2014, pp. 67-68.
4. The references to gups (or ranks) in Tang Soo Do is taken from the 1976 *Manual For Gups* by the U.S. Tang Soo Do Moo Duk Kwan Federation, Inc. and from the 2013 *Tang Soo Do Student Handbook* by Central Michigan Karate Club.